A SHEAF OF
STUDIES

A SHEAF OF STUDIES

BY

SIR EDMUND KERCHEVER CHAMBERS

Essay Index Reprint Series

BOOKS FOR LIBRARIES PRESS
FREEPORT, NEW YORK

STANDARD BOOK NUMBER:

8369-1398-1

LIBRARY OF CONGRESS CATALOG CARD NUMBER:

74-99622

PRINTED IN THE UNITED STATES OF AMERICA

PREFATORY NOTE

HERE are gleanings from a period of fifty years, largely devoted to activities other than literature. "The Poetry of Matthew Arnold" was a Warton Lecture before the British Academy. "Some Dates in Coleridge's *Annus Mirabilis*" was one of the "Essays and Studies" by members of the English Association. "Meredith's Nature Poetry" and "Alice Meynell's *Rhythm of Life*" were contributed to *The Academy*. "The Dedicated Life" was a lecture at Abercromby House in the University of Liverpool. "The Study of English Literature" was an Introduction to a school-book published by Messrs. Blackie & Son, Ltd. "The Timelessness of Poetry" was a Presidential Address to the English Association. "Ghosts in the Bodleian" was read at a meeting of the Friends of the Bodleian. "Oxford Revisited" appeared as "Ghosts" in *The Pelican Record*, the journal of my College of Corpus Christi, Oxford. My gratitude is due to all those who originally gave hospitality to these studies. "Matthew Arnold's Tree" and "Meredith's *Modern Love*" have not been printed before. War-time forbids a dedicatory page. I can, therefore, only record here how much this book, like all my literary work, owes to the sympathy and patience of my wife.

December, 1941.   E. K. C.

CONTENTS

MATTHEW ARNOLD'S TREE

THE DOG-ROSES were glorifying the hedges with their deepest red, when last, on 9th June, 1939, I stood by the gates of Chilswell Farm, and my thoughts turned once more to the achievement of that characteristic Oxford quest, the identification of the Tree in *Thyrsis*. This has been the subject of much journalistic controversy over a long period of years.[1] Three systematic attempts to trace the line of the walk which is the framework of the poem, and thereby to arrive at the Tree, have left me unconvinced.[2] I do not know whether I shall be more successful with a fourth, but at any rate it may as well go down upon paper, for what it is worth.

Arnold himself has left us little to go upon. Arthur Hugh Clough, who is Thyrsis, died at Florence on 13th November, 1861. "I shall some day in some way or other relieve myself of what I think about him", Arnold wrote to his mother on 20th November.[3] A few days later, on 30th November, he took occasion, in a lecture on Homer at Oxford, to commemorate "the Homeric simplicity" of his friend's literary life.[4] But it is not until 25th April, 1863, that we hear of the possible emergence of a poem. He had meant to begin it at Oxford that week, but "a detestable cold wind" had prevented him. He had, however, "been accumulating stores for it". On 7th April, 1866, he wrote that it had been forming itself, with the help of much reading of Theocritus,

---

[1] *Oxford Magazine*, 21st October–9th December, 1903; 15th November, 1905; 17th November–8th December, 1910; 1st May, 1913; 26th May–16th June, 1913; 26th May–16th June, 1938; *The Times Literary Supplement*, 1st–22nd November, 1917; 18th March–22nd April, 1939.

[2] A. D. Godley, *O.M.* 28th October, 1903, reprinted in *Reliquiae* (1926) i.165; Sir Edward Poulton, *The Signal-Elm in Thyrsis* (1911, *John Viriamu Jones and Other Studies*, 291); Sir Francis Wylie, *The Scholar-Gipsy Country* (1940, C. B. Tinker and H. F. Lowry, *The Poetry of Matthew Arnold*, 351).

[3] G. W. E. Russell, *Letters of Matthew Arnold* (1895), i. 152.

[4] H. F. Lowry, *Letters of Matthew Arnold to A. H. Clough* (1932), 160; *On Translating Homer* (ed. 1896), 177.

during two years. More than one walk, in the course of that period, may have contributed to it. But the last is likely to have been towards the end of November or early in December, 1865. On 18th November he was preparing lectures for Oxford in London.[1] I do not know on what days they were given, but term ended that year on 18th December.[2] By 3rd February, 1866, he had decided to publish the poem in *Macmillan's Magazine* for April, and there it duly appeared, just a fortnight, as I like to remember, after I was born.[3] It was reprinted in the *New Poems* of 1867, with some slight alterations, of which only one is significant. To that I shall have occasion to return.

Arnold leaves Oxford, I think, by Jacob's Ladder over the reservoir, and the "causeway chill", already recorded in *The Scholar-Gipsy*, which crosses the water-meadows to South Hinksey. He notes the changes of time in the two Hinkseys, and in particular the loss of a "haunted mansion" and of "Sibylla's name" from the sign of the inn, and then emerges at the top of the village on the way from the Oxford and Abingdon road to North Hinksey, once the scene of Ruskin's experiments in road-making, and now largely merged in a modern by-pass.[4] He does not follow this way, but crosses it to a "pathway" striking to the south-west, which at first mounts steeply, then becomes for a considerable space a level terrace, and finally descends into the "Happy Valley", a meadow fringed on its eastern side with trees, in which lies Chilswell Farm.[5] This is Arnold's immediate objective.

> Runs it not here, the track by Childsworth Farm,
>   Past the high wood, to where the elm-tree crowns
>   The hill behind whose ridge the sunset flames?
>   The signal-elm, that looks on Ilsley Downs,
>   The Vale, the three lone weirs, the youthful Thames?

At the top of the path he can turn, and have his retrospect of

[1] Russell, i. 191, 311, 325.   [2] *University Calendar* (1865).   [3] Russell, i. 315.
[4] Sir Michael Sadler tells me that Sybella Curr was buried at South Hinksey. She died in 1860.
[5] Not "Childsworth," as Arnold has it. The earliest (thirteenth century) forms of the name are Chiefleswell and Cheveleswell. The farm was once a manor, held on a military tenure under the Abbey of Abingdon.

the "lovely" city of Oxford, "with her dreaming spires", lying behind and below him. But as he proceeds on his way, a hesitation overtakes him, is he going in the right direction?

> Some loss of habit's power
> Befalls me wandering through this upland dim.
> Once pass'd I blindfold here, at any hour;
> Now seldom come I, since I came with him.
> That single elm-tree bright
> Against the west—I miss it! is it gone?
> We prized it dearly; while it stood, we said,
> Our friend, the Gipsy-Scholar, was not dead;
> While the tree lived, he in these fields lived on.

Then comes a long passage, the core of the poem, on the abandonment of the Gipsy-Scholar life, by himself, and more deliberately by Clough, on Clough's death, and on a contrast with the fate of Dorian shepherds, whom a song to Proserpine might bring back from the dead.

> But ah, of our poor Thames she never heard!
> Her foot the Cumner cowslips never stirr'd;
> And we should tease her with our plaint in vain!

> Well! wind-dispersed and vain the words will be,
> Yet, Thyrsis, let me give my grief its hour
> In the old haunt, and find our tree-topp'd hill!
> Who, if not I, for questing here hath power?

Presumably, if he has stopped for these reflections, he now walks on, with further musings on the beauty of the Oxford country in the past, on the deadening of emotion with advancing years, and on the loss of his friend. And then an incident breaks the train of his thought.

> But hush! the upland hath a sudden loss
> Of quiet!—Look, adown the dusk hill-side,
> A troop of Oxford hunters going home,
> As in old days, jovial and talking, ride!
> From hunting with the Berkshire hounds they come.
> Quick! let me fly, and cross
> Into yon farther field!—'Tis done; and see,
> Back'd by the sunset, which doth glorify
> The orange and pale violet evening-sky,
> Bare on its lonely ridge, the Tree! the Tree!

> I take the omen! Eve lets down her veil,
>   The white fog creeps from bush to bush about,
>   The west unflushes, the high stars grow bright,
>   And in the scatter'd farms the lights come out.
>   I cannot reach the signal-tree to-night.

He calls on his friend to share the omen with him.

>   Hear it, O Thyrsis, still our tree is there!—
>   Ah, vain! These English fields, this upland dim,
>   These brambles pale with mist engarlanded,
>   That lone, sky-pointing tree, are not for him.

Thyrsis is with the mighty mother in a boon southern country. But for himself the poet will not despair.

>   Despair I will not, while I yet descry
>   Neath the mild canopy of English air
>   That lonely tree against the western sky.

It is a token that the quest which the friends once shared with the Gipsy-Scholar is not dead. His haunt is still here, in

>   this rude Cumner ground,
> Its fir-topped Hurst, its farms, its quiet fields.

He bids Thyrsis share his confidence.

>   The light we sought is shining still.
>   Dost thou ask proof? Our tree yet crowns the hill,
> Our Scholar travels yet the loved hill-side.

I have isolated from the web of the poem its references to the Tree and its setting. But how far has the walk taken Arnold before the Tree breaks upon him? Probably he has at least descended the path from the ridge above South Hinksey, traversed the meadow in the Happy Valley, and reached Chilswell Farm at its head. From this point three ways diverge. To the north-west one, called by Sir Edward Poulton the "field-road", starts from the western side of the farm, runs under the lee of Henwood and its outlier Powder-hill Copse, to the left of the track, passes the bluff of Cumnor Hurst, still on the left, and joins the road from Oxford to Cumnor near Chawley Farm. To the south-east a continuation of the same field-road runs up to an outlier of Bagley Wood, and there joins the road from Oxford through Foxcombe to Boar's Hill. This is properly a hamlet in the parish of Wootton, although the use of the name has recently been extended to cover the whole of the populous area of Foxcombe above Tommy's Heath, much of which is really in the parish of Sunningwell. To the south-west of Chilswell Farm, a footpath climbs an open slope, once perhaps, as traces of ridge and furrow suggest, arable, but now grassy, and for some time used as part of a golf-course.[1] At the top of the slope the path meets a hedge, running nearly due south, passes through a wicket-gate, and now becomes a bridle-road, which leaves Pickett's Heath farm on its right hand, and emerges into the Oxford road near Boar's Hill proper. If, however, instead of going through the wicket-gate, you turn down the western side of the hedge enclosing the old golf-course, you find yourself opposite a tree, the second from the top of the hedge, which stands in another field beyond it.[2] It has in fact become visible as you mounted the slope, and is very conspicuous from the bridle-road, just beyond the wicket-gate. It does not, strictly speaking, crown the hill, as the poem requires, since the ground drops again rather steeply down the hedge. But it appears to do so from a distance. This, according to a fairly early Oxford tradition, is the Tree of *Thyrsis*. It is not an elm, but an oak, although the growth of its upper branches was abnormal for an oak, and much resembled that of an elm. From this appearance it has been called the " Umbrella" tree. Much of the upper growth has now gone, and the elm-like shape is less obvious. But it can be seen in some photographs taken by Mr. H. W. Taunt, about the beginning of the present century.[3]

The tradition to which I refer seems first to have taken recorded form in Mr. G. C. Druce's *Flora of Berkshire*, published in 1897, just about thirty years after the poem

[1] Field 41 (496). I cite field numbers from the Ordnance Survey of 1913, and add in brackets those given by Sir Edward Poulton from that of 1876.

[2] Field 23 (87).

[3] *The Oxford Poems of Matthew Arnold ... with ... Rambles with Matthew Arnold.* Neither the original edition nor an abridgement published by Alden and Co. bears a date. But the Oxford City Librarian tells me that he believes the first to date about 1915.

appeared in print. Here, in an account of *Ulmus*, Druce wrote:

> Matthew Arnold alludes in *Thyrsis* to a tree that grows nearly on the summit of the Boar's Hill range, which is a prominent object from the Ridgeway.

And after quoting some lines from the poem, he added:

> But the tree which is now associated with Matthew Arnold is really an oak of a somewhat unusual shape, reminding one rather of the Italian Pine.

This is rather ambiguous. Intervening woodland screens the Boar's Hill area from the Ridgeway, and I take it that the first tree described by Druce was that on Cumnor Hurst, to which I shall come later. The Hurst is very conspicuous from the railway, as it passes under the Ridgeway near Didcot. Druce's second tree is no doubt the "Umbrella" tree. But it is not clear which tree Druce himself, in 1897, believed to be Arnold's. Challenged for his evidence in 1903, Druce gave the name of the Rev. William Tuckwell of Lincoln College, who liked to be known as the "Radical Parson". Tuckwell had now written to him.

> Uncritical acceptance of tradition fixed the umbrella-tree for me. When *Thyrsis* came out in the Sixties, men walking on the Iffley Road, then unobscured westward, used always to point to the tree and quote the lines, and so I hold to the belief with the tenacity of a mind habitually incredulous.[1]

Tuckwell had been familiar with Oxford from his boyhood, and ought to have been an authority on its traditions. In his *Reminiscences of Oxford* (1900) he wrote of Arnold's leap over the Wadham railings [now gone], which was familiar to many who had never read his books, and of Arnold and Clough as "mounting to the Glanvill elm, which yet stands out clear against the flaming sunset sky".[2] There is, of course, a confusion of thought here. There is an elm in Joseph Glanvill's *The Vanity of Dogmatizing* (1661), from

[1] *Oxford Magazine*, xxii, 139.
[2] *Reminiscences* 97, 110. Tuckwell's disordered correspondence in *Bodl. S. Top. Oxon* b. 164 seems to add nothing.

which Arnold took the theme of *The Scholar-Gipsy*, and none, except the Fyfield elm, in *The Scholar-Gipsy* itself.[1] Druce returned to the subject in 1910, now dating Tuckwell's statement to him in 1879, and adding that a projected excursion with Tuckwell and Arnold himself to visit the ground had never matured, owing to the poet's death in 1888. He now brought confirmatory testimony to the umbrella-tree from George Simms, once a bootmaker in the Broad, who knew Arnold, and W. F. Baxter, the custodian of the Botanic Garden and the Parks.[2] This is further evidence of the tradition, which is in any case undisputed, but I doubt whether a reticent Arnold confided in his bootmaker. Finally, in 1913, Tuckwell reiterated his adherence to the umbrella-tree, adding that he had only learnt from Druce in 1910 that it was an oak.[3]

The tradition has received support from a belief that Arnold himself had confirmed it in conversation. But for this I find no conclusive evidence. In 1910 Mr. P. H. Lee-Warner wrote that he had asked many contemporaries and even familiar friends of the poet which was the tree, but that none could give him a categorical answer.[4] According to L. R. Phelps, at one time Provost of Oriel, Arnold, when questioned, was rather annoyed, but said that the tree could be seen from the railway, which would fit the umbrella-tree. The bold enquirer was at first believed to have been R. G. Tatton, known to my contemporaries as the Balliol "dancing don" from one of Dr. Mackail's epigrams. But this turned out to have been a mistake. In 1911 surviving members of Arnold's family could contribute no "decisive memories". Sir Edward Poulton believed that J. R. Thursfield had the identification from Arnold's brother, Thomas.[5] There could be no more likely recipient of a confidence than the "dear old Tom" of the poet's letters, who was in fact walking with him by the Cherwell in February, 1866.[6] But a statement

---

[1] A theory in *T.L.S.* (18th March and 1st April, 1939) derived from Philip Bliss, once sub-librarian at the Bodleian, that the tree was the Fyfield elm itself, is negligible. The Fyfield tree is separately mentioned in *Thyrsis*.

[2] *Oxford Magazine*, xxix, 138.   [3] *Ibid*. xxxii, 299.

[4] *Ibid*, xxix, 88.   [5] Poulton, 292.   [6] Russell i. 319.

by Thursfield himself brings some qualification of this testimony.[1] Thomas Arnold had in fact told him that he had himself always accepted the umbrella-tree as that of *Thyrsis*, "but he did not, so far as I can recall, cite the poet's own authority for the identification". Mowbray Morris added a touch of humour to the legend by declaring that Arnold had told him that the tree was a "morella" tree.[2] There is much of the gossip of an Oxford common-room in all this. More important is a statement by the late Professor A. C. Bradley, who pointed out that the umbrella-tree can be seen from the train, a little before it enters Oxford Station from the south, and added:

> About 1877 I asked Matthew Arnold whether the tree thus visible was the Tree of *Thyrsis*, and he answered without hesitation 'Yes'.[3]

This might seem conclusive, were it not for an impression that Matthew Arnold was inclined to assent with urbanity to any interpretation of the poem that was offered to him. Certainly A. C. Bradley's statement conflicts with the recollection of his much older half-brother, G. G. Bradley, formerly Master of University College, Oxford, a life-long friend of Arnold's from Rugby days, and one of the earliest admirers of *Thyrsis*.[4] This tradition was thus reported in 1929 by his daughter, Mrs. Margaret Woods, the poetess.

> The ridge of Boar's Hill—the ridge of *Thyrsis*—is completely transformed by building; but before that happened the view of it from Oxford had been gradually altered by the growth of trees. About the centre of the view fifty years ago a single tree stood up against the sky, prominent only because it stood alone. Many a time I have looked up from Oxford and seen it black against the sunset and my father has told me that this was the Tree of *Thyrsis*. It stood beside what was then a sandy track and is now a road. At a distance it resembled an elm, but in fact it was an oak. This was a detail which, my father said—would easily have escaped Matt. The topographical objection that from this particular point you cannot see the 'three lone weirs' mentioned in the poem—I myself have never been able to determine which they are— he dismissed for similar reasons.[5]

Mrs. Woods had already made use of the Tree and its

[1] *T.L.S.* (8th November, 1917).   [2] *Oxford Magazine* (9th June, 1938).
[3] *T.L.S.* (22nd November, 1917).   [4] Russell i. 325 (7th April, 1866).
[5] *Essays and Studies* (English Association) xv, 19.

"sandy track" in her novel *The Invader* (1907), and more recently she has been good enough to confirm her account in letters both to me and to the late Warden of New College, Dr. H. A. L. Fisher. She cannot now find the tree, and believes that it must have been cut down. It was quite an insignificant tree in itself, made only remarkable by its solitary position on what was then a bare ridge, along which Mrs. Woods had often ridden as a girl. "It stood by a gate just opposite what was our stable-yard gate, when we lived in the house where Ripon Hall now stands." It was "not umbrella in shape". Ripon Hall is on the road from Oxford to the hamlet of Boar's Hill, and this must, I think, have been the "sandy track" of which Mrs. Woods writes. I have been unable to discover from local records the date at which it was made up into a firm road, but I seem to recall it as still a mere track in my own youth. The bridle road from Chilswell Farm past the umbrella-tree to Boar's Hill is, however, also a "sandy track". But if the tree near Ripon Hall has now gone, Mrs. Woods must have been under a misapprehension in 1903, when she thought it might have been that on the old golf-course, as to the position of which she was not clear, and again in 1911, when she assented to Sir Edward Poulton's argument in favour of the tradition.[1] The traditional tree still stands, and is very conspicuous as you look down from the Boar's Hill road, not far from Ripon Hall, a little before you reach Tommy's Heath. Probably, however, it was this, and not the one near Ripon Hall, to which Mrs. Woods used to look up from Oxford itself. There is, I may add, still a very fine oak at the gate of Ripon Hall.

Some other trees in the neighbourhood of Boar's Hill and Pickett's Heath have been suggested as possibly Arnold's.[2] I cannot identify them, and I doubt whether they have any advantage over those already mentioned. I turn, therefore, to Sir Edward Poulton's considered defence of the tradition. He supposes Arnold, as I do, to leave Oxford by South Hinksey and the footpath above it. And this brings him up

[1] *Oxford Magazine*, xxii, 46.
[2] Godley, *Reliquiae* i. 165; *T.L.S.* (15th November, 1917); *Oxford Magazine* (9th June, 1938).

at once against a serious initial difficulty. The umbrella-tree would have been plainly visible from an early stage of the walk, firstly at the crossing over Jacob's Ladder, and secondly, for a considerable time, during the traverse of the level terrace at the top of the footpath. Sir Edward is aware of this, but he gets over it by suggesting, without any help from the poem itself, that Arnold was pondering over old associations in *reverie*, and failed to notice the tree. I do not think that this is very good psychology. The perceptions of poets are acute; it is in pondering over them afterwards that they become transmuted into poetry. Perhaps, Sir Edward allows, Arnold thought of the tree when he reached the Happy Valley at the bottom of the descent, but here the trees on the left of the path would screen it from him.[1] And so too it would be, when he passed into the space on the south of the farm, where is the juncture of the two field-roads and the way to Boar's Hill.[2] As a matter of fact, I think that the slope of the old golf-course would by itself be sufficient to conceal the tree from this point. But surely the "signal-elm" had come into Arnold's thoughts at a much earlier stage in the walk. It is first mentioned in the second stanza of the poem, just before the reflection on the beauty of Oxford, which he presumably turned round to regard from the top of the ridge above South Hinksey. If it were the umbrella-tree, could he possibly have remained oblivious, as he proceeded along the level terrace, that he had it in full view? Yet in the third stanza he says, "I miss it! is it gone?" Some other tree than that before his eyes must be in his mind.

However, Sir Edward Poulton supposes the whole long passage of reminiscences and reflection which follows, broken only by a resolve to find the "tree-topped hill", to be spoken while the poet is still standing in front of Chilswell Farm. It ends with the sudden appearance of the troop of Oxford hunters going home. They would be coming, according to Sir Edward, by the path down the grassy slope from the Boar's Hill bridle-road, and would be making either for that by which Arnold himself had come, or more probably for the field-road to Bagley Wood, from which the Abingdon

---

[1] Field 54 (492).   [2] Field 41 (496).

and Oxford road could be reached. The poet decides to evade them.

> Quick! let me fly, and cross
> Into yon farther field!

He does so, and as a result gets his vision of the Tree. His exact movements, says Sir Edward, were as follows. He walked seventy-five yards to a gate over the field-road, and up the field-road for another forty-five yards along the edge of a field on his left.[1] Then he turned through the gate of another field on his right, and twenty more yards across this would bring him within sight of the tree, while fifty would give him a really fine view of it.[2] It would be a little more than half a mile away, and it would be too late on a November evening for him to reach it. Sir Edward's reconstruction is topographically accurate, as the ground now stands. In fact, if Arnold had looked to the right, as he went through the gate over the field-road, he would have found another gate, and over it got a sight of the tree, without more ado. Nor am I quite sure that, even in winter, half a mile need have prevented him from reaching it. Possibly, however, some gateless hedge may have intervened. One cannot, of course, be sure, that there has been no alteration in the lay-out of the fields since Arnold's day, perhaps on the abandonment of the golf-course. Certainly there is now a third field-road, shown in the Oxford Preservation Society's map, which runs from the same point of juncture as the others, but in a more southerly direction. Perhaps it is a more pertinent criticism that, in view of the lie of the land, the hunters must have been fairly near Arnold when he caught sight of them, and that, if you want to evade an oncoming troop of horsemen, your natural instinct is to move, not along a line which they are likely to take, but at right angles to that line, and that if Arnold had done this, by passing between a pair of trees and mounting the grassy slope, he would soon have found himself within easy distance of the tree.

Sir Edward Poulton's theory of Arnold's movements, if you forgive him his initial *reverie*, is no doubt a coherent

[1] Field 50 (500).   [2] Field 45 (499).

one. But there remain two very serious obstacles to the
tradition. The first is the obvious one that the umbrella-
tree is not an elm, but an oak; the other that it does not
even stand at the top of its own ridge, and that you cannot see
from it the three lone weirs or the Vale of White Horse, if
that is the Vale intended, although you might possibly get a
glimpse of the Ilsley downs through a gap in the Foxcombe
woodland to the south. The same difficulty, I fear, attaches
itself to the vanished tree on the road to Boar's Hill, and
indeed to any tree in that neighbourhood. The mass of Henwood entirely blocks any view of the upper Thames valley.
Sir Edward brushes away this criticism.

   Both difficulties are at once removed, if we accept the probable
view that the poet did not investigate, but based his statements on the
general appearance of the tree and its position.

So, too, Druce had written before him, "The power of
generalisation is a poetic license." It is not, however, exactly
generalisation to turn an oak into an elm. We have here, of
course, examples of the normal attitude of the man of science
towards the mere men of letters. They are a dreamy folk,
with no faculty for exact observation. It has little application
to Arnold, for whom in poetry, as in criticism, it was a cardinal
virtue to keep an eye on the object. He had, in fact, long
been something of a botanist. His letters are full of references
to trees and plants which he had noticed, to the Turk's
Caps in the Oxfordshire meadows, to the campanulas by the
Thames near Laleham, to the Westmoreland flowers, the
buckbean, asphodel, whortleberry, which he found again in
Belgium, to the gentians and rhododendrons in the Alps,
more relevantly to the pollarded elms on the Middlesex plain,
and the pollarded oaks of Brittany.[1] One mistake he made, in
The Scholar-Gipsy. He described the Convolvulus minor as
blue, and corrected it to pink in a later edition. Of his own
poems he wrote, early in 1856, that there are those to whom
"the literalness and sincerity of them has a charm"; and of
Thyrsis itself in 1866 that "the images are all from actual
observation."[2] I do not see how he can have taken an oak

[1] Russell, i. 3, 74, 82, 85, 120, 191.   [2] Russell, i. 51, 325.

for an elm, or described a tree he knew well as looking upon
what it could not see.

A. D. Godley's interpretation of Arnold's walk diverges
at an important point from Sir Edward Poulton's. According
to him, the poet did not linger at Chilswell Farm, but turned
along the north-western field-road towards Cumnor Hurst
and Chawley. This runs for some way between the ridge
above North Hinksey on the right and Henwood and its outlier Powderhill Copse on the left. These were familiar haunts
of my own youth, pursuing *lepidoptera* with Arthur Sidg-
wick of beloved memory. We were not too literary to be
able to distinguish oak leaves from elm leaves in gathering
provender for caterpillars. I do not know why the authorities
of the Oxford Preservation Trust thought this beautiful
valley a suitable line along which to bring electricity cables
to the city. It may well be here that, according to the poem,
the "track by Childsworth Farm" runs "past the high wood".
Originally, in *Macmillan's Magazine*, the phrase was "up
past the wood". Sir Edward claims this in favour of his
theory, because the path to Boar's Hill rises, with a bit of the
woodland to the right of it. But I think that the argument
runs the other way. Arnold improved the line—it was his
one significant alteration in 1869—for greater " literalness".
According to Godley, the walk followed this field-road, up
to a point where it is joined on the left hand by a bridle road
running down from the Faringdon road near Besselsleigh
and the Rockley cottages, and passing between Powderhill
Copse and Cumnor Hurst on its way to North Hinksey.
Here it was that Arnold met the hunters descending, and at
about the same suddenly saw his tree on the Hurst itself, with
the sunset behind it. Sir Edward Poulton rejects this theory
on two grounds. One is that an experienced horseman had
told him that he had often come home from a hunt by the
Boar's Hill bridle-road, but never by Henwood Farm, which
lies between Besselsleigh and the Hurst. That does not seem
to me very material. The line, which a hunter would follow,
to get home to Oxford after a hunt, would depend entirely
upon where the kill did, or did not, take place, and from some
points in the Berkshire country he might very naturally go

through North Hinksey. Sir Edward's second criticism is that the tree, when seen, is "backed by the sunset", and that the winter sunset is so far to the south that, from Godley's suggested station, is would seem to be at right angles to the Hurst, and just over the path by which Godley takes the hunters to be descending. That is true, but the spread of a winter sunset often extends far on either side of the apparent point of sinking, and it is Arnold himself who describes the tree as seen "against the western sky".

A recent study of the poem by Sir Francis Wylie offers yet another solution of the problem. He, too, believes in the umbrella-tree.

And what if the tree *is* an oak, not an elm? For Arnold, this tree was just a feature in the landscape, a landmark, a 'signal-tree'. I question whether either he or Clough ever thought to ask what sort of tree it was. Twenty years later, it was just a tree seen from far off; and who that knows the tree will be so bold as to say that, so seen, it proclaims itself—to the layman at any rate—an oak? Not, I think, to many.

That would have been all very well, if Arnold had merely called the tree a tree, but unfortunately he twice calls it an elm. And I have already pointed out that he was by no means a layman in botany. Sir Francis, however, agrees with me that it would hardly have been possible to escape seeing the umbrella-tree from the top of the South Hinksey ridge. And he suggests that the poet did not reach Chilswell Farm by that route at all, but went from South Hinksey to North Hinksey, and thence by a way above the village, itself part of the old packhorse track from Oxford to Besselsleigh, which would bring him down to the same point on the field-road to Chawley, as that indicated by Godley, but from a different direction. He is not strictly accurate in saying that here the packhorse road enters Powderhill Copse. There is a foot-path into the copse, but the packhorse road runs up outside its north-western edge. At the point, however, where it crosses the field-road, Arnold, according to Sir Francis, was driven by the approach of the hunters to turn along the field-road itself in the direction of Chilswell Farm.

And, as he moved that way, a field or two further on, the Tree, hidden before by a bulging hillside, will have come suddenly into view, against the glow of a winter sunset.

I have an impression that I have myself seen the umbrella-tree from such a point, but I am not quite certain. Possibly the trees of Birch Copse were not high enough to intervene. But here again, even more than in Godley's case, how about the sunset? The tree would now be, not to the west or even to the south-west of the walker, but to the due south of him. It is true that Sir Francis Wylie's theory as to the line of the walk would give more point to the mention of "the two Hinkseys" at the beginning of the poem, and also that the "haunted mansion", which was lacking from the village street, may have been one which once stood, but stands no longer, in North Hinksey, for although South Hinksey had also its ghost, in one Jenny Bunting, the "Parlour" which she haunted was apparently not a mansion, but an old quarry.[1] On the other hand Sir Francis is making the poet take an extremely roundabout way by which to reach Chilswell Farm in a short winter afternoon. Even if he wished to pass by "Arnold's field" above North Hinksey, which enshrined the memory of his father, but which he does not mention in the poem, it would have been quicker to leave Oxford by the Botley road and cross over by Hinksey Ferry.

I adhere, in the upshot, to the line of walk indicated by Godley, as far as the point of the meeting with the hunters. But I do not believe with him that the tree was on Cumnor Hurst itself. There was a very fine elm there, but it was not "lone", as the poem requires, since it stood only about thirty-five feet from a big clump of firs. It has been suggested that the firs were of later growth than the date of the walk.[2] They are, however, recorded in 1824.[3] The poem itself, indeed, has an independent mention of the "fir-topped Hurst". Moreover, the top of the Hurst would have been fully in Arnold's view, except so far as some unusually tall hedge might intervene, during nearly the whole of the walk along the field-road from Chilswell Farm. It could not

[1] H. W. Taunt, in *The Oxford Poems of Matthew Arnold* (n.d.), 32.
[2] *Oxford Magazine*, xxii, 46.
[3] J. W. Burgon, *The Lives of Twelve Good Men*, ii. 115.

suddenly break upon him at the point indicated by Godley. Nevertheless, I feel sure that Godley was upon the right line, when he looked in the direction of Cumnor. The "Cumner cowslips" and "this rude Cumner ground" are in the poem itself. I do not know why Arnold meticulously substituted this spelling for "Cumnor" in 1869, but it is that usual in his letters. In *The Scholar-Gipsy* again, although there is some mention of Bagley Wood and its outlier Thessaly, it is the Cumnor hills which the wanderer mainly haunts. And if you turn to the letters, you find nothing of Boar's Hill or its neighbourhood, but a remarkable emphasis on the poet's enduring affection for Cumnor. The references to it begin as early as 1849 in a letter to Clough himself.[1]

Not deep the Poet sees but wide—think of this as you gaze from the Cumner Hill toward Cirencester and Cheltenham.

So to his wife in 1854.[2]

I am going with Walrond to-day to explore the Cumner country, and on Thursday I got up alone into one of the little coombs that papa was so fond of and which I had in my mind in the 'Gipsy Scholar', and felt the peculiar *sentiment* of this country and neighbourhood as deeply as ever.

To his brother Thomas in 1855.[3]

What you will like best, I think, will be the 'Scholar Gipsy'. I am sure that old Cumner and Oxford country will stir a chord in you.

To Thomas again in 1857.[4]

Do you remember a poem of mine called 'The Scholar Gipsy'? It was meant to fix the remembrance of those delightful wanderings of ours in the Cumner hills before they were quite effaced—and as such Clough and Walrond accepted it.

To his mother in 1861.[5]

Presently I am going to my old haunts among the Cumner hills, and shall come back with plenty of orchises and bluebells.

To Mrs. Clough in 1862.[6]

I cannot tell you how glad I am to have the lines you have sent me.

[1] Lowry 99.　　　　　　　　　　　　　　[2] Russell, i. 38.
[3] Mrs. H. Ward, *A Writer's Recollections*, 53.　　　[4] *Ibid.*
[5] Russell i. 135.　　　　　　　　　　　　[6] Lowry, 160.

I shall take them with me to Oxford, where I shall go alone after Easter; and there, among the Cumner hills where we have so often rambled, I shall be able to think him over as I could wish.

To his mother in 1863. [1]

The weather was fine, but with a detestable cold wind, so that a new poem about the Cumner hillside, and Clough in connection with it, which I meant to have begun at Oxford this week, I could not begin. I have been accumulating stores for it, however.

To J. C. Shairp in 1866. [2]

'Thyrsis' is a very quiet poem, but I think solid and sincere. It will not be popular, however. It had long been in my head to connect Clough with that Cumner country, and when I began I was carried irresistibly into that form; you say, truly, however, that there is much in Clough (the whole *prophet* side, in fact) which one cannot deal with in this way, and one has the feeling, if one reads the poem as a memorial poem, that not enough is said about Clough in it; I feel this so much that I do not send the poem to Mrs. Clough. Still Clough *had* this idyllic side, too; to deal with this suited my desire to deal again with that Cumner country: anyway, only could I so treat the matter this time. *Valeat quantum.*

To his mother in 1870. [3]

I had a walk with Tom up towards my old Cumner country on Sunday.

To J. D. Coleridge in 1882, on *Westminster Abbey*. [4]

If it is inferior to 'Thyrsis', that may be because the scene of 'Thyrsis' is laid in that Cumner country which moves my affections so much.

To his family in 1885. [5]

On Friday I got out to Hinksey and up to the hill to within sight of the Cumner firs. I cannot describe the effect which this landscape always has upon me—the hillside with its valleys, and Oxford in the great Thames valley below.

---

[1] Russell, i. 191.   [2] Russell i. 326.   [3] Russell ii. 32.
[4] E. H. Coleridge, *Life of J. D. Coleridge*, ii. 309.
[5] Russell ii. 286.

It is always Cumnor that pulls at Arnold's heartstrings. There is not a word of Boar's Hill or Foxcombe. But on Cumnor Hurst itself it is the firs he notes, not an elm.

If then the Tree was not on the Hurst, where was it? When I first went to live at Eynsham in 1927, and was coming and going on my lawful occasions between that place and the Bodleian, I was constantly much struck by a magnificent elm, with widely spreading branches, which stood alone, in the midst of cornfields, on a high slope, to the south of my road, between Cumnor village and Chawley Farm.[1] Could this possibly be the elm of *Thyrsis*? I repeated Godley's walk from Chilswell towards the Hurst, and when I came to the point where he supposed Arnold to have met the hunters, looked for a "farther field", into which to fly. There was an obvious one, across the line of the packhorse track from Besselsleigh, on the ridge of the Hurst itself, not at its summit, where the firs stand, but lower down, on its shoulder. It was easily accessible over a fence, and mounting it I was rewarded by seeing the Chawley elm just below me. The ground falls steeply here, and to ascertain what view would be visible from the tree, it was necessary to turn back, pass round the bluff of the Hurst and emerge by the Chawley tile-works. This may well have been too far for Arnold, when the west unflushed and the high stars grew bright. I had doubted whether the tree stood high enough to give the required view. But it did. There was the Vale, not of the White Horse, but of the Upper Thames, and even, rather to my surprise, a glimpse, on a clear day, of the Downs, although, I should think, rather nearer Lambourn than Ilsley. In the farther distance, you could look away, as Arnold's letter to Clough has it, "toward Cirencester and Cheltenham". The "three lone weirs" were not individually discernible through my field-glasses. Eynsham weir is hidden behind Beacon Hill at the head of the Wytham ridge. The three must, I think, have been Pinkhill weir, Skinner's weir and the Ark or Noah's Ark weir above Bablock Hythe. All three still stood in 1878,

[1] Field 144.

but Skinner's weir was removed in 1880, and the spot is now only marked by a bridge.[1]

I am still a little troubled by A. C. Bradley's conversation with Arnold. But Bradley's memory was not his strongest point, in his later years. And there may have been some misunderstanding, perhaps conscious on Arnold's side, between them. You could see the Chawley elm from the railway, not however from near Oxford, but near Eynsham. And of course, it is open to the same objection which Sir Edward Poulton brought against the elm on the Hurst, that the November sun, as seen from my point on the Cumnor ridge, would not set exactly behind it. But in any case, no one will again see it, as Arnold saw it, against the north-western spread of the glow. The Tree fell in the great gale of 8th December, 1929, and by an odd coincidence the elm on the Hurst also fell in that same night of havoc. Perhaps it was as well. The Chawley field is now a building estate. On 9th June, 1939, the stump of the tree was still there, with a forest of young elm saplings growing up around it. But small houses had already crept down to within a few yards of it. It may have been uprooted by now. Better so, perhaps, than that it should remain in a back-garden, as a convenient thing on which to hang out the family washing.

Cedit enim rerum novitate extrusa vetustas.

1941.

----

[1] H. W. Taunt, *Map of the Thames* (1878). I owe the date for the end of Skinner's weir to the kindness of the Thames Conservancy. Pinkhill weir was the *gurges* of William de Puntle, more probably Puncle, as far back as 1302 (v. my *Eynsham Under the Monks*, 27, 67, 81).

THE POETRY
OF MATTHEW ARNOLD

MATTHEW ARNOLD is now, I suppose, like most of his contemporaries, a natural target for the shafts of post-war criticism. I have read a book about him, the writer of which appears to have taken his inspiration from the insolent grace of Mr. Lytton Strachey, and to have succeeded admirably in catching the insolence. I shall say no more about it. In this company, I hope that I speak to many impenitent Victorians like myself, who still find in that bygone verse the cool refreshment which it breathed upon its first readers, in days which seemed to Matthew Arnold feverish enough, although they were far less feverish than our own. *Virgilium vidi tantum.* I have a boyhood's image of an Olympian figure, moving somewhat aloof on the outskirts of an Ambleside garden-party; and it was in the week in which I first came up as a freshman that Arnold paid his last visit to Oxford, staying with Thomas Fowler of genial memory in my own college of Corpus, and took his last walk in the happy coombes of Hinksey.

The chronology of the poems is rather difficult. It appears to have been Arnold's habit to let things lie aside for some time after they were written, and even when they had been published to drop and revive them, and arrange and rearrange them, according to the shifting moods of his critical taste. The Rugby and Oxford prize poems he never admitted to the canon, but the earliest pieces therein contained must have come soon after the Newdigate of 1843. One of them was the sonnet on Shakespeare, of which an autograph copy is dated 1844. The lines *To a Gipsy Child* were written on a visit to the Isle of Man in 1845. Both of these appeared in Arnold's first volume, named from *The Strayed Reveller*, of 1849. This probably only had a small circulation, and before the year was out, Arnold wrote that he had "got absolutely to dislike it". A second volume of 1852, which included

Tristram and Iseult, was withdrawn out of dissatisfaction with its title-poem, *Empedocles on Etna.* Most of the contents of both volumes were gradually reissued, with other work, old and new, in small gatherings of 1853, 1854, 1855, and 1857. The *New Poems* of 1867 gave the vintage of another decade. A fairly complete collection of 1869 restored some things that had been lost. But its order was only tentative, and that of the current editions dates from a recast of 1877. Here most of the pieces from the volume of 1849 and a few from those of 1852 and 1853 are relegated to a category of *Early Poems,* and as the rest of the classification is by "kinds" of poetry, a good deal of cross-division is entailed. The critical estimate of a life-work of poetry depends so much on chronology that it would not be unreasonable for a writer who arrives at a collective edition, while following what arrangement he thinks fit, to label each piece with its date. As it is, one cannot, I think, in the case of Arnold, rely upon the propinquity of poems, at any stage of publication, as evidence either of a common date or of a common inspiration. An exception must of course be made for a few which are brought together in groups under comprehensive headings.

In those groups we are met on the threshold by the enigmatic figure of Marguerite. There are nine poems which were definitely written around Marguerite. All but one name her, in text or title, and about that one there can be no doubt. Eight of them were gradually issued from 1849 to 1857; one, *The Terrace at Berne,* which appeared in 1867, was professedly an epilogue, written after an interval of ten years. All nine, at one time or another, found a place in the group called *Switzerland,* which was differently composed in 1853, 1854, 1869, and 1877. Two, *A Memory Picture* and *A Dream,* are now separated from the rest, and put among the *Early Poems.* These nine poems, taken by themselves, sufficiently shadow out a story. It is one of an attraction passing into a passion, of doubt and reluctance from the beginning, of a growing sense of incompatibility on both sides, of a parting which, for a time at least, presented itself as a tragedy, a tragedy inevitable because it was based on character:

> A God, a God their severance ruled!
> And bade betwixt their shores to be
> The unplumb'd, salt, estranging sea.

The poet is left with a bitter sense of isolation, which he takes as a law of existence for him, and perhaps in some measure for all men. As he turns away, a consciousness of his own nature and vocation, which has beset him throughout, brings into the utterance of his "vainly throbbing heart" an undertone akin to relief. A sterner life than that of this alluring dream has long been his lot:

> Farewell!—and thou, thou lonely heart,
> Which never yet without remorse
> Even for a moment didst depart
> From thy remote and spherèd course
> To haunt the place where passions reign—
> Back to thy solitude again!
>
> Back! with the conscious thrill of shame
> Which Luna felt, that summer-night,
> Flash through her pure immortal frame,
> When she forsook the starry height
> To hang over Endymion's sleep
> Upon the pine-grown Latmian steep.
>
> Yet she, chaste queen, had never proved
> How vain a thing is mortal love,
> Wandering in Heaven, far removed.
> But thou hast long had place to prove
> This truth—to prove and make thine own:
> "Thou hast been, shalt be, art, alone."
>
> Or, if not quite alone, yet they
> Which touch thee are unmating things—
> Oceans and clouds and night and day;
> Lorn autumns and triumphant springs;
> And life, and others' joy and pain,
> And love, if love, of happier men.
>
> Of happier men—for they, at least,
> Have *dream'd* two human hearts might blend

In one, and were through faith released
From isolation without end
Prolong'd; nor knew, although no less
Alone than thou, their loneliness.

Many of the earlier poems, besides *Switzerland*, must be put, wholly or in part, to the account of Marguerite. I think we are bound to give her the five which were gathered into the group called *Faded Leaves* in 1855. And there are several others in the volume of 1852 and a few even in that of 1849 which either directly concern her, or at least, like *The New Sirens*, echo the spiritual issues which his relations with her raised in Arnold's mind. There are hints of her, beyond the name Margaret, in *The Forsaken Merman*, and again in *Tristram and Iseult*, both in the main theme and in the Merlin and Vivian story at the end. I do not dissent from Professor Garrod when he calls the volume of 1852 "Marguerite's book, the book of forsaken or separated lovers". But I think that he is inclined to press the point rather far. She is not the only woman in the book. I cannot find her reflected in Urania, who has seen through the hearts of men, and whose

lovely eyes maintain
Their pure, unwavering, deep disdain.

There was mockery in Marguerite's eyes, but it was the mockery of tenderness, not of disdain. And it is surely fantastic to suppose that a morbid imagination of her death inspired the *Lines Written on a Death-Bed*, to which one would certainly have to add the *Requiescat* of 1853. This was the death-bed of a tired woman, who had known fear and shame, and whose face bore the ravages of time. But Marguerite is ever fresh and young, and her feet flit lightly down the flowery track. It is true that Arnold did once, in *The Terrace at Berne*, long after she had passed out of his life, have the thought that she might be dead, but only to reject it:

Could from earth's ways that figure slight
Be lost, and I not feel 'twas so?
Of that fresh voice the gay delight
Fail from earth's air, and I not know?

Or shall I find thee still, but changed,
But not the Marguerite of thy prime?
With all thy being re-arranged,
Pass'd through the crucible of time;

With spirit vanish'd, beauty waned,
And hardly yet a glance, a tone,
A gesture—anything—retain'd
Of all that was my Marguerite's own?

I have written as if Marguerite were a real woman, and I find it hard to believe that it is not so. I am aware of the tradition handed down in Arnold's family that he had declared her to be imaginary; and no doubt one must give full value to any statement made by a middle-aged poet in reply to the questionings of his daughters about the object of his early love lyrics. And no doubt, too, imagination has played its part. But the poems do at least leave the impression of a very definite and vivid personality, with many details which are not essential to the emotional theme, and give an air of verisimilitude. Marguerite was a daughter of France. She was literate enough to lend Arnold a volume of the *Letters of Ortis*, a sentimental romance by the Italian poet Ugo Foscolo. She dwelt in a steep street by the Aar, near the "roof'd bridge that spans the stream" and the twin lakes. It is clearly Thun. She had a housemate, Olivia; the names may of course have been altered. She had a slight figure, an arch smile, an exquisite voice, a "pale sweet-rounded cheek". A kerchief commonly enwound her hair. Several of these intimate touches recur again and again. They do not suggest a figure of drama. The only possible inconsistency is in colouring. In *Parting* Marguerite has "soft, ash-colour'd hair"—*blond cendré* one supposes, rather than the black of Tennyson's ashbuds in March. Her eyes are normally blue. But in *Absence* a "stranger's eyes of grey" recall them, and in *Separation*, one of the *Faded Leaves* group, there is a wish that she may be wholly forgotten, and at some future meeting,

Who, let me say, is this stranger regards me,
With the grey eyes, and the lovely brown hair?

Between brown and ash-coloured, however, we need not dispute, and although eyes are a point on which lovers ought to be clear, it is not always so. Perhaps we may call in aid another of the *Faded Leaves* poems, which has

> Eyes too expressive to be blue,
> Too lovely to be grey.

Even so Swinburne writes of—

> Those eyes the greenest of things blue,
> The bluest of things grey.

There can have been no mystery about Marguerite in the Arnold family at the time, although personal references have been rather carefully cut out of such of the poet's letters as have yet been published. *Absence*, however, was read to one of his sisters just after it was composed, and Arnold reminds her, a quarter of a century later, how she had been touched by it.

As to the date of the Marguerite episode, we cannot at present be quite certain. The only poem which names her in the 1849 volume is *A Memory Picture*, the first of the *Switzerland* series, and that is written in a lighter tone than the rest. But here is also to be found *The Voice*:

> So sad, and with so wild a start
> To this deep-sober'd heart,
> So anxiously and painfully,
> So drearily and doubtfully,
> And oh, with such intolerable change
> Of thought, such contrast strange,
> O unforgotten voice, thy accents come,
> Like wanderers from the world's extremity,
> Unto their ancient home!
>
> In vain, all, all in vain,
> They beat upon mine ear again,
> Those melancholy tones so sweet and still.
> Those lute-like tones which in the bygone year
> Did steal into mine ear—
> Blew such a thrilling summons to my will,
> Yet could not shake it;

> Made my tost heart its very life-blood spill,
>   Yet could not break it.

I agree with Professor Garrod that this can only be one voice, the voice of Marguerite in *The Terrace at Berne*, her voice in *Parting*:

> But on the stairs what voice is this I hear,
> Buoyant as morning, and as morning clear?
> Say, has some wet bird-haunted English lawn
> Lent it the music of its trees at dawn?
> Or was it from some sun-flecked mountain-brook
> That the sweet voice its upland clearness took?

And if so, the closing lines of *The Voice* seem to make it clear that the episode was already over when that poem came to be printed in 1849. A date in 1848 is just possible, but one in 1847 or earlier is more likely. I ought to add that I have quoted a revised text of 1877. That of 1849 has, among variants of a more literary character, "long-distant years" for "the bygone year", and "long sober'd heart" for "deep sober'd heart". I do not much believe in "long distant years" which would take us back to Arnold's boyhood. It is conceivable that there was some *camouflage* in 1849, and that in these points the text of 1877 is the original one. The Berne poem ought to help in the dating, but I am not sure that it does. In the collection of 1869 it stood at the end of the *Switzerland* group, with a note that it was "composed ten years after the preceding". Arnold was at Berne in 1865, and the last of the earlier *Switzerland* poems was printed in 1855. But the words of the poem itself would suggest that the lapse of ten years had been since the parting. Arnold's letters record several visits to Switzerland towards the end of the 'fifties, but none that clearly took him to Berne. I think that 1857 is a possibility, because he then wrote of "two or three things I have in hand, which I cannot finish till I have again breathed and smelt Swiss air". But Berne would have entailed some alteration of his planned itinerary.

I make no apology for being curious about Marguerite. The first love of a poet can never be without interest, or without significance. But I do not want to inquire too closely how much in the lyrics she evoked is a literal transcript from experience, and how much grew up round that experience when it was in fact over. These are delicate things to handle.

Tread softly, because you tread on my dreams.

If I am right as to the dates, there was time between 1849 and 1852 for the "shaping spirit of imagination" to have play. Certainly the parting with a blue-eyed girl became for Matthew Arnold something more than itself, a parting with the whole world of passionate romance which he put behind him. The Marguerite poems are not merely poems of isolation, but of renunciation, of self-dedication. There had been a κάθαρσις. He turned back to his "spheréd course", to the rigorous teachers who had seized his youth, to

The dragon-warder'd fountains
Where the springs of knowledge are,

and incidentally to the routine, which he often found irksome, of the Education Office. But these early poems have a lyric plangency, which is not quite the note of those that followed.

Poetry, indeed, he did not lay aside, but for a time it took a more impersonal form, on classical models which were always dear to him. By 1853 he was at work upon *Sohrab and Rustum*, which appeared later in the year with the famous preface, in which Arnold laid down that "the eternal objects of Poetry, among all nations, and at all times" are "actions; human actions; possessing an inherent interest in themselves, and which are to be communicated in an interesting manner by the art of the Poet". This was consonant enough with his own mood when it was written. But it is a curious limitation of the scope of high poetry, the criterion of which, on the side of impulse, as distinct from craftsmanship, is surely to be found, not in the nature of its subject matter, but in the quality of the emotional excitement which that subject matter, whether a human action or some simple fact of observation, or feeling, or reflection, has aroused in the mind of the poet. Matthew Arnold has said many sound things about poets and poems, and in particular about poetic diction, but I do not think that he was ever at his best in attempting to expound the fundamental basis of poetic activity. He comes nearer to the truth in a much later essay, at the point where, after exalting Wordsworth over other poets because he deals with more of life, and deals with it, as a whole, more powerfully than they do, he is suddenly taken aback at finding himself in apparent agreement with the logical but eminently prosaic mind of Leslie Stephen. Wordsworth's poetry was great, according to Leslie Stephen, because his philosophy was sound. "No," says Arnold, "Wordsworth's poetry is great because of the extraordinary power with which Wordsworth feels the joy offered to us in nature, the joy offered to us in the simple primary affections and duties; and because of the extraordinary power with which, in case after case, he shows us this joy, and renders it so as to make us share it." But I am not here to discuss Matthew Arnold as a critic. He wrote *Sohrab and Rustum*, with "more pleasure than anything I have done yet". And it is a noble poem, the fruit of his constant preoccupation with Homer, whose works, he says, for one or two years, were seldom out of his hands. But it is no mere transcript from Homer. It is Homeric in its large utterances, its forthrightness, its constant use of expanded similes; un-Homeric and modern in its concentration on a theme of family relationship such as Homer only lightly touches, in the more conscious elaboration of its decorative passages, and above all in the enveloping presence of the river Oxus, which is a recurrent note throughout, and culminates in the magnificent *finale*, too familiar for me to quote, where the father and the son are left alone on the darkling plain, and the Oxus, regardless and serene, moves onward to the Aral sea. *Sohrab and Rustum* was followed by *Balder Dead*, of which Arnold remained proud, thinking that it had "a natural propriety of rhythm and diction", which he found in Virgil, and did not, in after thought, altogether find in *Sohrab and Rustum*. The verse has dignity, no doubt, and there are some good similes, and one very beautiful and characteristic one, in which the touch of a brother in the dark is

As a spray of honeysuckle flowers
Brushes across a tired traveller's face

Who shuffles through the deep dew-moistened dust,
On a May evening, in the darken'd lanes,
And starts him, that he thinks a ghost went by.

But few will put the poem, as a whole, on a level with its predecessor. Its theme, indeed, hardly satisfies Matthew Arnold's own requirements for poetic narrative. Here is no excellent human action, where the shadowy figures of a priestly mythology are impelled by unintelligible motives to inconclusive ends.

During the next decade, Arnold's poems came slowly, although, as gathered in the volume of 1867, they form a substantial body, of unimpaired poetic quality. They close, indeed, with the *Thyrsis* of 1866, which is perhaps his finest single work. But educational duties pressed upon him throughout, and in 1857 the Professorship of Poetry turned his thoughts to prose. Probably his poetic impulse never flowed easily. Over *Thyrsis* itself he brooded long. Clough, on whom it was in part written, died in 1861. Arnold had meant to begin it at Oxford in the spring of 1863, but was prevented by "a detestable cold wind". He could do no more, he wrote, than accumulate stores for it. In the same letter he notes the fritillaries in the meadows by the Thames. All the images in *Thyrsis*, he said later, were from actual observation. The cuckoo, however, was heard, not at Hinksey, but at Woodford, in Epping Forest, during 1864. The poem, therefore, took at least two or three years in the making. There is much evidence that at all times in this decade Arnold found the writing of poetry difficult. Another letter, of 1858, is in the nature of an *apologia* for *Merope*. It was motived by the temptation "if you cannot bear anything not *very good*, to transfer your operations to a region where form is everything". A kind of perfection might thus be approached. But to attain perfection in thought and feeling, as well as in form, seemed to him impossible, "unless one can devote one's whole life to poetry", as Wordsworth, Shelley, Byron, and Tennyson were able to do. Probably Matthew Arnold was carrying too great a load of competing activities. But I do not myself believe in the doctrine of a complete dedication to poetry. Poetry is, after all, the reflex of life, and life, if its reflex is to be of value, must be lived for itself. It is remarkable how much of the world's greatest poetry has in fact been written by men who largely spent themselves in normal occupations, and, on the other hand, how dilute the poetry of live-long poets has often become. Wordsworth is an outstanding example of this. It is no part of my object to attempt a comparison between the best work of Matthew Arnold and that of his six greatest contemporaries. Personal taste and emotional sympathy inevitably play too great a part in any such estimate. But one may fairly maintain that the *proportion* of work which endures is greater in the case of Matthew Arnold than in that of any one of them. Nevertheless it is true that in middle life he came more and more to feel poetry slipping away from him, and that for this his preoccupations were at least in part responsible. More than once he resolved to lay critical writings aside and return to the Muses. "The period between forty and fifty", he wrote in 1861, "is not a bad ten years of one's life for poetry, if one resolutely uses it, but it is a time in which, if one does not use it, one dries up and becomes prosaic". One does, no doubt. But his hopes were not to be realized. Forty saw him plunged in educational controversy, and on the eve of those long inquiries into the conditions of foreign schools, which were destined to have so profound an ultimate influence upon the development of education in this country. And these in their turn were followed by the remarkable essays on the trend of English civilization, social and religious, which have done more than we always realize to determine our modern apprehension of spiritual values. Matthew Arnold's poetic activity practically closed with the volume of 1867. Even so, twenty years was a reasonable span. As it happens, it was just that of Shakespeare's poetic life, and of Spenser's. The Destinies gave Shelley no more than twelve, and Keats no more than five. Wordsworth's poetic life, rightly measured, was about ten. Perhaps Arnold recognized the inevitable, when he issued his collection of 1869. It was not quite complete. One of the omitted poems was *The Voice*, in which he detected a tone of falsetto. I do not myself feel that there is much falsetto, if by that is meant the kind of thing which you get in *Maud* and *Locksley Hall*, and some other of the less successful attempts of Tennyson. But Arnold was always fastidious. One or two other poems were more or less re-written. The texts of the rest do not differ substantially from the earlier ones. But there was a good deal of touching up, generally for the better, in small details of craftsmanship. Clashes of sound and repetition of epithets were eliminated. Arnold, like meaner men, was occasionally worried by the difficulty of securing the right alternation of "that" and "which". And there are some amusing alterations due to the increased knowledge of field botany which he acquired in his later years. The original blue convolvulus on the stubble field of *The Scholar-Gipsy* becomes a pink one. The reaping scene of *Bacchanalia* is turned into a mowing scene, because the dog-rose is over before harvest time. The "green fern" of *Tristram and Iseult* gives place to "last year's fern", because that is what you really get in April. Another example of Arnold's desire for literal fidelity of visual rendering is also to be found in *The Scholar-Gipsy*. Instead of "the slow punt swings round" he put "the punt's rope chops round". It is less elegant, but the punt at Bablock-hythe is so fixed as to make a moving bridge which cannot swing round. Arnold lived for nearly twenty years after the collection of 1869 was issued. Even to the end he was still occasionally wondering, rather wistfully, whether he should ever do anything more in poetry. "It is something", he adds, "to have been of use in prose". And so, indeed, it is. The occasional pieces, mostly elegies on household pets, of these later years, although grace-fully turned, do not amount to much. But I must own that I should like to know what became of the *Lucretius*, which Arnold long had by him, and evidently never finished. It must be the "tragedy of the time of the Roman Republic", which he was full of in 1855, but did not expect to have ready before 1857. In 1866 he was perturbed by hearing that Tennyson was at work on the story of Lucretius, and thought that a common friend must have suggested the subject. He had himself been occupied with it for twenty years. He meant to go on, but could not publish before the following year. A month later four lines from *Lucretius, an unpublished Tragedy*, were prefixed to *Thyrsis* as it first appeared in *Macmillan's Magazine*. They are not reprinted in the *Collected Poems*, and I will quote them.

> Thus yesterday, to-day, to-morrow come,
> They hustle one another and they pass;
> But all our hustling morrows only make
> The smooth to-day of God.

Writing to F. T. Palgrave in 1879, Arnold again named *Lucretius*, as one of the things which he would like to do in poetry before he died, and of which lines and bits had long been done. The subjects of the others were St. Alexius and the journey of Achilles after death to the island of Leuce. "But", he adds, "we accomplish what we can, not what we will."

I turn to another aspect of Matthew Arnold's poetry. The elegiac temper pervades it from beginning to end, and it is perhaps this, rather than the exaltation of the early lyric, or the deep harmony of *Sohrab and Rustum*, which seems to the modern reader his peculiar characteristic. The elegy, as is common with elegy, often has an idyllic setting. *The Scholar-Gipsy* and *Thyrsis* we all know, but let me quote in illustration from two shorter poems. The first is *Resignation*, which is early:

> He sees the gentle stir of birth
> When morning purifies the earth;
> He leans upon a gate and sees
> The pastures, and the quiet trees.
> Low, woody hill, with gracious bound,
> Folds the still valley almost round;
> The cuckoo, loud on some high lawn,
> Is answer'd from the depth of dawn;
> In the hedge straggling to the stream,
> Pale, dew-drench'd, half-shut roses gleam;
> But, where the farther side slopes down,
> He sees the drowsy new-waked clown
> In his white quaint-embroider'd frock
> Make, whistling, tow'rd his mist-wreathed flock—
> Slowly, behind his heavy tread,

> The wet, flower'd grass heaves up its head.
> Lean'd on his gate, he gazes—tears
> Are in his eyes, and in his ears
> The murmur of a thousand years.

The second is *Bacchanalia*, which is late:

> The evening comes, the fields are still.
> The tinkle of the thirsty rill,
> Unheard all day, ascends again;
> Deserted is the half-mown plain,
> Silent the swaths! the ringing wain,
> The mower's cry, the dog's alarms,
> All housed within the sleeping farms!
> The business of the day is done,
> The last-left haymaker is gone.
> And from the thyme upon the height,
> And from the elder-blossom white
> And pale dog-roses in the hedge,
> And from the mint-plant in the sedge,
> In puffs of balm the night-air blows
> The perfume which the day forgoes.

For such writing I will venture to borrow the phrase of a poetess who herself wrote no poetry, "It calls home the heart to quietness". The country dear to Matthew Arnold was very quiet country. Hinksey and Cumnor, the haunts of his youth and mine, to which he always returned on his visits to Oxford, were not what are called beauty spots. They were merely uplands of ancient pasture, down some of which, by the time of *Thyrsis*, the ploughboy's team had already gone; with a bit of woodland, a wide outlook over Oxford itself and the surrounding valleys, and little footpaths running from farm to farm beneath high hedges. You may taste such quietness in any part of England still, if you care to leave the roadways. Arnold has other scenery as well; that of the Lake Country, that of a Surrey common, with its hollies, in *Tristram and Iseult*, that of the lower Alps, where the yellow gentian flames on the way to

> Jaman, delicately tall,
> Above his sun-warm'd firs;

that of Sicily in *Empedocles on Etna*, with its classical reminiscences. It is all quiet. From all alike he draws the cool
refreshment of which I have already spoken. You will find,
if you run through the poems, that "cool" is his favourite
epithet. And above all he loves the coolest things in the world,
the dew at morning and in the evening, and the moon. How
many of his best things are drenched in moonlight! The
Merman creeps to shore,

> When clear falls the moonlight,
> When spring-tides are low.

In *The Youth of Nature*,

> The lake,
> Lovely and soft as a dream,
> Swims in the sheen of the moon.

The Scholar-Gipsy has its "moon-blanched green", *Dover
Beach* its "moon-blanch'd land", *A Summer Night* its "moon-
blanch'd street"; and both this and *A Southern Night* recall
an unforgotten experience in which the moon had its part:

> And to my mind the thought
> Is on a sudden brought
> Of a past night, and a far different scene.
> Headlands stood out into the moonlit deep
> As clearly as at noon;
> The spring-tide's brimming flow
> Heaved dazzlingly between;
> Houses, with long white sweep,
> Girdled the glistening bay;
> Behind, through the soft air,
> The blue haze-cradled mountains spread away,
> The night was far more fair—
> But the same restless pacings to and fro,
> And the same vainly throbbing heart was there,
> And the same bright, calm moon.

The moon, again, shines on Tristram's death-bed, and
through the clerestory windows of *The Church of Brou*. The
Oxus flows through the hushed Chorasmian waste "under
the solitary moon". Apollo and the Muses in *Empedocles*
roam through the "moon-silver'd inlets" of Thisbe vale.

The nightingale of *Philomela* sings in the moonlit cedar. The full moon lights the "groups under the dreaming garden-trees" in *Thyrsis*. The quietness of Arnold's vision is enhanced by the quality of his verse; its simplicity, lucidity, and straightforwardness; its literalness, I think he would have said; the sparing use of aureate words, or of far-fetched words, which are all the more effective when they come; the avoidance of inversions, and the general directness of syntax, which gives full value to the delicacies of a varied rhythm, and makes it, of all verse that I know, the easiest to read aloud. Here are some at least of the characteristics which Arnold found in Homer and did not find in some of Homer's translators. But it was only in *Sohrab and Rustum* and *Balder* that he essayed the Homeric grandeur. The diction of *Thyrsis* he says, was modelled on that of Theocritus. He felt that it was "a very quiet poem".

As a poet of natural beauty Matthew Arnold is the direct inheritor of Wordsworth. He acknowledges the derivation more than once; in *The Youth of Nature* and in the *Memorial Verses*:

> He laid us as we lay at birth
> On the cool flowery lap of earth,
> Smiles broke from us and we had ease;
> The hills were round us, and the breeze
> Went o'er the sun-lit fields again;
> Our foreheads felt the wind and rain.
> Our youth return'd; for there was shed
> On spirits that had long been dead,
> Spirits dried up and closely furl'd,
> The freshness of the early world.

And like Wordsworth, the Wordsworth of "The world is too much with us", he contrasts the quiet of nature with the disquietude of man,

> This iron time
> Of doubts, disputes, distractions, fears,

the "benumbing round", the "faded, ignoble lives" of world-lings, the

> Strange disease of modern life,
> With its sick hurry, its divided aims.

He looks upon

> The long heart-wasting show,
> Wherein earth's great ones are disquieted.

Man is "the eternal trifler":

> We see all sights from pole to pole,
> And glance, and nod, and bustle by,
> And never once possess our soul
> Before we die.

The thought is more habitual than in Wordsworth. And indeed the parallel between Wordsworth and Arnold must not be pushed too far. They differed both in temper and in conviction. We have seen that what Arnold felt most clearly in Wordsworth's reaction to nature and life was joy. But the poet of *Resignation*, written around those fells of Watendlath which Wordsworth knew so well, has another outlook. He too, as he leans on his gate in the misty morning, sees the whole of life unroll before him, just as Wordsworth might have done. But for him it is a life

> Whose secret is not joy, but peace.

And again:

> Yet, Fausta, the mute turf we tread,
> The solemn hills around us spread,
> This stream which falls incessantly,
> The strange-scrawled rocks, the lonely sky,
> If I might lend their life a voice,
> Seem to bear rather than rejoice.

Nor were the spiritual implications in Wordsworth's matured poetry of nature such as Arnold could accept. Content as a boy to take "the harvest of a quiet eye", or at the most, in retrospect at least, shot through from time to time with dim intimations of unknown modes of being, Wordsworth found his way to a conviction, based on mystic intuition rather than logical reasoning, of a universal harmony in things. The life of man is bound up with the life of nature, and together they are the vehicle of a power that informs them both. This doctrine finds its clearest expression in the lines on *Tintern*

Abbey. Ultimately Wordsworth gave it a more specifically Christian turn.

> I have felt
> A presence that disturbs me with the joy
> Of elevated thoughts: a sense sublime
> Of something far more deeply interfused,
> Whose dwelling is the light of setting suns,
> And the round ocean, and the living air,
> And the blue sky, and in the mind of man:
> A motion and a spirit, that impels
> All thinking things, all objects of all thought,
> And rolls through all things.

This philosophic optimism, if the term is not too intellectual a one to use, was never Matthew Arnold's. His rigorous teachers had purged his faith, and shown him "the high, white star of Truth", and in that clear and searching light he could see no certainty of such a harmony. His prevailing elegiac mood is one of disequilibrium. He can arrive at no coherent vision of the scheme of things entire. Nature follows the course of nature, and man follows the course of man. Between these there may be contacts. Man may learn endurance as well as peace from nature, when

> With joy the stars perform their shining,
> And the sea its long moon-silver'd roll.

It is the lesson of the sonnet on *Toil and Tranquillity*, which once stood at the head of his first volume. The "sleepless ministers" of nature are the "labourers that shall not fail, when man is gone". But what assurance is there that even the reasonable strivings of men serve a divine end? We strive to little purpose:

> Unbreachable the fort
> Of the long-battered world uplifts its wall.

And we strive blindly:

> We are here as on a darkling plain
> Swept with confused alarms of struggle and flight,
> Where ignorant armies clash by night.

Once again the sense of isolation is strong upon him. At the best we are "in some unknown Power's employ". Arnold stood too near his lost faith to become a contented pagan. He feels as one adrift from his moorings. He envies the Scholar Gipsy, in his single-eyed chase, year after year, of a constant aim,

> Still nursing the unconquerable hope,
> Still clutching the inviolable shade.

He envies the calm security of the Carthusian in his cell, regardless of the banners and the bugles of the outer world:

> Like these, on earth I wait forlorn.
> Their faith, my tears, the world deride—
> I come to shed them at their side.

But the "cloister-floor of humid stone" is not for him; and indeed he would have been ill at ease on it.

> The Sea of Faith
> Was once, too, at the full, and round earth's shore
> Lay like the folds of a bright girdle furl'd.
> But now I only hear
> Its melancholy, long, withdrawing roar,
> Retreating, to the breath
> Of the night-wind, down the vast edges drear
> And naked shingles of the world.

It is possible to lay too much emphasis upon this side of Arnold's poetry. That is an error of perspective into which, I think, some of his critics have fallen. After all, the elegies only represent one factor in a complex personality, reacting from strenuous days of unfaltering devotion to the service of what is best in humanity. Arnold was no Obermann, sadly watching the irretrievable flux of things from the door of his high chalet on the green slopes of Jaman. The pulse of living in him was too strong for that stern withdrawal and its "hourly varied anodynes". To that "unstrung will" and "broken heart" he bade farewell, with much else, when he returned to his "sphered course". A visit to Glion brought an hour of recollection:

> An eremite with thee, in thought
> Once more I slip my chain.

But although Obermann had been "the master of my wandering youth", he had then been "left for many a year". One must not expect to find consistency in the moods of a poet. Often enough, natural beauty seems to be for Arnold a mere *refrigerium*. But it is not always so. There is at least meliorism, if not optimism, at the end of *Obermann Once More*, as the dawn breaks over the Valais; and again in *The Future*, where the river of Time, in "wider, statelier" flow, may yet strike peace to the soul of humanity,

> As the stars come out, and the night-wind
> Brings up the stream
> Murmurs and scents of the infinite sea.

Nor is the tonic strain of "unresting, unhasting" endeavour a rare one. It is something more than mere acceptance; rather the spirit of morality suffused by emotion which Arnold found in Marcus Aurelius, "a spirit not so much of gladness and elation, as of gentleness and sweetness; a delicate and tender sentiment, which is less than joy and more than resignation". It informs, very notably, the musings over the example of Arnold's own father in *Rugby Chapel*. The testament of Empedocles to Pausanias does not show the poet's thought at its clearest, or give it its finest expression, but here too is such consolation as a stoic may take. Life has a bounty for man, if he will only be moderate in his demands on it:

> Is it so small a thing
> To have enjoy'd the sun,
> To have lived light in the spring,
> To have loved, to have thought, to have done;
> To have advanced true friends, and beat down baffling foes?
>
> I say: Fear not! Life still
> Leaves human effort scope.
> But, since life teems with ill,
> Nurse no extravagant hope:
> Because thou must not dream, thou need'st not then despair.

And this is echoed, long after, in the sincerity and simplicity of *A Wish*. The poet would have no doctor at his death-bed, and no "brother-doctor of the soul", no whispering crowded room, no air of ceremony.

> Bring none of these; but let me be,
> While all around in silence lies,
> Moved to the window near, and see
> Once more, before my dying eyes,
>
> Bathed in the sacred dews of morn
> The wide aerial landscape spread—
> The world which was ere I was born,
> The world which lasts when I am dead;
>
> Which never was the friend of *one*,
> Nor promised love it could not give,
> But lit for all its generous sun,
> And lived itself, and made us live.
>
> There let me gaze, till I become
> In soul, with what I gaze on, wed!
> To feel the universe my home;
> To have before my mind—instead
>
> Of the sick room, the mortal strife,
> The turmoil for a little breath—
> The pure eternal course of life,
> Not human combatings with death!
>
> Thus feeling, gazing, might I grow
> Composed, refresh'd, ennobled, clear;
> Then willing let my spirit go
> To work or wait elsewhere or here!

The wish was only half fulfilled. It is a little ironical, and more than a little pathetic, that Matthew Arnold, the apostle of quiet, died running to catch a tram.

Matthew Arnold's tree, the "lone sky-pointing" elm of *Thyrsis*, fell in one of the great gales of December, 1929. It is not quite certain where it stood. The late A. D. Godley wrote a paper in which he traced very conclusively the course which Arnold must have taken on the footpath from Childsworth Farm to the neighbourhood of Cumnor Hurst, and came to the decision that the elm must have been that on the top of the Hurst. I believe it myself to have been one which was reached a little farther along the same line of walk. It was a noble tree, which stood, "bare on its lonely ridge", in the great field between Chawley Farm and Cumnor village, a good deal lower than the Hurst, but with the same double prospect of the Berkshire Downs and the Upper Thames Valley. And it was solitary, whereas the tree on the Hurst was close to the ring of firs which gives its main character to that eminence. It matters little now, since both trees fell in the same night of wreck. Cumnor still keeps its incommunicable secret. In the grassy harvest of the Eynsham water meadows the fritillaries blow no longer. And now we must believe that the Scholar Gipsy has ceased to roam those slopes. His quest was bound up with the life of the tree. Already there are spots near Cumnor which he could not wish to haunt. And I gather that the bridle track from Appleton, down which the troop of Oxford hunters came in *Thyrsis*, is marked out by the industrial masters of our destiny for a range of electric pylons. When I last trod the Childsworth footpath its serenity was undisturbed. A single wayfarer was crossing it towards an opening in "the high wood". He stooped, and may have been a scholar. But he was not the Scholar Gipsy, for he was pushing a bicycle. Immortal, like mortal things, touch the mind in their perishing.

1931.

SOME DATES IN COLERIDGE'S
ANNUS MIRABILIS

COLERIDGE'S own dates for the ballads of his flowering time at Stowey were recorded long after they were
written. His editors, James Dykes Campbell in 1893 and
Ernest Hartley Coleridge in 1907 and 1912, have occasionally departed from them, on a theory that in such points his
normal "tenacious and systematizing" memory was apt to
fail him. "Coleridge is generally unreliable in the matter of
dates assigned to particular single events", writes Campbell,
and this is echoed by Professor Lowes with "The one thing
which Coleridge seems to have been constitutionally incapy-
ably of remembering correctly was a date that concerned himself".[1] I am not sure that the facts cited by Professor Lowes
fully bear out so sweeping a statement. There is a constant
error as to the day, and sometimes the year of his birth, which
was hardly within the scope of his own memory. Probably he
had not consulted the Ottery registers. There is a tendency
to ascribe undated scraps of verse to his schoolboy days.
There are two definite misdatings in books printed away from
his eye in 1815, for an unsatisfactory publisher, one of which
he repeats in a letter of the same date. I will not claim that he
was infallible.

The important issue, of course, is as to the time-relations
of *The Ancient Mariner* and *Christabel*. In reviewing the
somewhat complicated evidence, I will begin from the angle
of an unnamed ballad which figures in Coleridge's correspondence of 1797–8. It is first mentioned in an undated
letter to his friend and publisher, Joseph Cottle of Bristol.[2]
The manuscript is mutilated, but the earlier part of the letter
appears, from the fragment preserved, to have been devoted,

---

[1] J. L. Lowes, *The Road to Xanadu* (1931), pp. 356, 584.
[2] Harvard College Library, 19478. 5. F. I owe a photostat to the kindness
of Professor Lowes.

wholly or mainly, to criticism of a poem by Southey. Then Coleridge turns to his own affairs.

I am translating the Oberon of Wieland—it is a difficult Language, and I can translate at least as fast as I can construe.—I pray you, as soon as possible, procure for me a German-English Grammar—I believe, there is but one—*Widderburne's*, I think—but I am not certain.—I have written a ballad of about 300 lines—& the Sketch of a Plan of General Study:—and I have made a very considerable Proficiency in the French Language, and study it daily—and daily study the German—so that I am not, and have not been, idle.— —I have heard nothing about my Tragedy, except some silly remarks of Kemble's, to whom Linley shewed it—it does not appear to me that there is a shadow of probability that it will be accepted.——It gave me no pain—& great pleasure in finding that it gave me no pain. I had rather hoped than believed, that I was possessed of so much philosophical capability.—Sheridan, most certainly, has not used me with common Justice. The proposal came from himself—and altho' this circumstance did not bind him to accept the Tragedy, it certainly bound him to pay every & that the earliest, attention to it. I suppose, it lies snugly in his green Bag—if it have not emigrated to the Kitchen or the Cloāca.

I sent three mock Sonnets in ridicule of my own, & Charles Lloyd's, & Lamb's, &c &c—in ridicule of that affectation of unaffectedness, of jumping & misplaced accent on common-place epithets, flat lines forced into poetry by Italics (signifying how well & *mouthisly* the Author would read them) puny pathos &c &c—the instances are almost all taken from mine & Lloyd's poems— —I signed them Nehemiah Higginbottom. I think they may do good to our young Bards.—
God love you &

S. T. Coleridge.

P.S. I have procured for Wordsworth's Tragedy an Introduction to Harris, the Manager of Covent-garden—who has promised to read it attentively and give his answer immediately—and if he accept it, to put it in preparation without an hour's delay.

Cottle's treatment of this letter is a characteristic example of the way in which he handled his Coleridge material, both in his *Early Recollections* (1837) and in its revised form as *Reminiscences of Samuel Taylor Coleridge and Robert Southey* (1847). He nowhere prints it as a whole. Most of it appears, very inaccurately, as an undated letter, inserted between notices of events of 1797 and 1798.[1] The bit about Words-worth's tragedy is given separately, some pages earlier.[2] That about the ballad and the plan of general study is put in 1795, with a hope that "the productions named may be still in existence".[3] The manuscript, however, is endorsed, probably by Cottle himself, as of "Nov. 1797", and internal evidence shows that this is approximately right. We know from other sources that Coleridge's *Osorio* was sent to the poet Bowles for transmission to Sheridan on 16th October, 1797;[4] that Wordsworth's *Borderers* had gone to Covent Garden by 20th November;[5] that the Higginbottom sonnets were in *The Monthly Magazine* for November, published in December;[6] that the rejection of *Osorio* had been notified by 2nd December;[7] and that Coleridge had been working during the last three months of 1797 on a "plan of general study" for a group of pupils to be taken in conjunction with Basil Montagu.[8] Sheridan's methods in dealing with business affairs were much like Coleridge's own, and the green bag into which he put unanswered letters was notorious. But even Coleridge could hardly have become impatient for a decision on his play much before the middle of November.

We hear next of a ballad on 6th January, 1798, when Coleridge wrote to Estlin on his plans for meeting his debts:[9]

I will sell my Ballad to Phillips who I doubt not will give me 5£ for it.

This was Richard Phillips, the proprietor of *The Monthly Magazine*, wherein, however, no such ballad is traceable. A third letter is again to Cottle, on 18th February, 1798.[10]

I have finished my ballad—it is 340 lines. I am going on with the Visions—all together (for I shall print two scenes of my Tragedy, as

---

[1] *E. R.* i. 288; *Rem.* p. 159.   [2] *E. R.* i. 251; *Rem.* p. 143.
[3] *E. R.* i. 138; *Rem.* p. 66.
[4] G. Greever, *A Wiltshire Parson* (1926), p. 32.
[5] W. Knight, *Letters of the Wordsworth Family* (1907), i. 112.
[6] iv. 374.
[7] E. L. Griggs, *Unpublished Letters of Coleridge* (1932), i. 84.
[8] *Letters to J. P. Estlin* (1884), p. 46.   [9] Griggs, i. 92.
[10] Griggs, i. 101.

fragments) I can add 1500 lines—now what do you advise? Shall I add my Tragedy and make a second volume? or pursue my first intention of inserting the 1500 in the 3rd Edition.

The "3rd Edition" never appeared. Nor was *Osorio* then printed. The two scenes from it are in the *Lyrical Ballads* of 1798. Here, too, is *The Ancient Mariner*, as a "Rime". In the second edition of 1800 it became, for a time, "A Poet's Reverie". It is, of course, in strict form a ballad. Wordsworth called it a "Vision".[1] But the "Visions" of the letter to Cottle were almost certainly the *Visions of the Maid of Orleans*, with which Coleridge originally meant to piece out his contribution to *Joan of Arc* for the *Poems* of 1797. He dropped them in deference to Lamb's criticisms, and never in fact finished them. The surviving fragments were printed as part of *The Destiny of Nations* in *Sibylline Leaves*.

It is reasonable to suppose that all three of Coleridge's letters refer to the same ballad. But can we identify it? There are four things which have to be taken into account—*The Ancient Mariner*, the First Part of *Christabel*, *The Dark Ladie*, *The Three Graves*.

Of *The Ancient Mariner* we hear nothing by name, until Cottle took it from Alfoxden to Bristol, probably in June, 1798, to begin the printing of the *Lyrical Ballads*.[2] When Coleridge revised it about 1815 for the volume which appeared as *Sibylline Leaves* in 1817, he added the note:

It was on a delightful walk from Nether Stowey to Dulverton, with him [Wordsworth] and his sister, in the Autumn of 1797, that this Poem was planned, and in part composed.

About the same date, describing in the *Biographia Literaria* the genesis "during the first year that Mr. Wordsworth and I were neighbours" of the *Lyrical Ballads*, he says that in accordance with the plan for this:

I wrote "The Ancient Mariner", and was preparing among other poems, "The Dark Ladie", and the "Christabel", in which I should have more nearly realised my ideal, than I had done in my first attempt.[d]

The chronology here is, of course, less precise than that of

---

[1] *Prelude*[1], xiii. 396.   [2] *E. R.* i. 315; *Rem.* p. 178.
[3] *B. L.* (ed. Shawcross), ii. 6.

Sibylline Leaves. The "year" in question may be, not a calendar year, but the period from 28th June, 1797, to 2nd July, 1798, during which the Wordsworths were at Stowey and Alfoxden. More puzzling is a later statement. On 22nd October, 1815, Coleridge sent to Lord Byron seventeen lines of verse as being all he could remember from a poem called *The Wanderings of Cain*, of which he had lost the only copy.[1] On 12th May, 1825, in response to a request for an autograph, he sent to an acquaintance, possibly T. J. Pettigrew, the same lines and title, and wrote at the top of the sheet, "The first stanza of the Poem, composed in the same year in which I wrote the Ancient Mariner and the first Book of Christabel".[2] The keen éye of Professor Lowes has observed that "year" is an alteration in the manuscript for "month". The same lines, with the same heading, were printed, also in 1825, as a footnote to *Aids to Reflection*.[3] To *The Bijou* (1828) Coleridge contributed, under the title of *The Wanderings of Cain: A Fragment*, not a poem, but a passage of prose narrative. This was also given in the *Poetical Works* of 1828, with a prefatory note, in which Coleridge ascribes the piece to 1798, and says that it was "to have been written in concert with another", clearly Wordsworth, and finished in one night; that he had drawn up a scheme and written the second "canto"; that his partner had broken down over the first; and that "the Ancient Mariner was written instead". "Years afterwards", he adds, "I determined on commencing anew, and composing the whole in stanzas", but did not complete it, and now could only recover the introductory stanza, which had been written down. Then follow the lines already printed in 1825. Obviously there is some confusion here. Coleridge must have been in error when he treated the verse as part of the original composition. That this was in prose we have the confirmation of Hazlitt, who visited the Valley of Stones at Lynton with Coleridge in June or July, 1798, and was told "that he and Wordsworth were to have made this place the scene of a prose tale, which was to have been in the manner of, but far superior

[1] Griggs, ii. 146.
[2] Harvard 19478. 5. F; cf. Lowes, p. 538.   [3] p. 383.

to the 'Death of Abel', but they had relinquished the design."[1] Some prose fragments contributed by E. H. Coleridge to the *Athenæum* of 27th January, 1894, seem to be part of Coleridge's preliminary "scheme". Even in 1828, however, Coleridge's memory must have slipped. His date of 1798 for *Cain*, "instead" of which *The Ancient Mariner* was written, is inconsistent with his date of 1797 for the beginning of *The Ancient Mariner* itself in *Sibylline Leaves.*

Wordsworth, too, had his reminiscences of *The Ancient Mariner.* In a passage of *The Prelude*, written, according to Professor de Selincourt, in May, 1805, he recalls to Coleridge:

> That summer when on Quantock's grassy Hills
> Far ranging, and among her sylvan Combs,
> Thou in delicious words, with happy heart,
> Didst speak the Vision of that Ancient Man,
> The bright-eyed Mariner, and rueful woes
> Didst utter of the Lady Christabel;
> And I, associate with such labour, walk'd
> Murmuring of him who, joyous hap! was found,
> After the perils of his moonlight ride
> Near the loud Waterfall; or her who sate
> In misery near the miserable Thorn.[2]

The summer was no doubt that of 1798, not 1797, since we known that *The Thorn* was written on 19th March, 1798. In 1843, dictating some notes on *We are Seven* to Miss Isabella Fenwick, Wordsworth said:

In the spring of the year 1798, he [Coleridge], my Sister, and myself, started from Alfoxden, pretty late in the afternoon, with a view to visit Linton, and the valley of Stones near it; and as our united funds were very small, we agreed to defray the expense of the tour by writing a Poem, to be sent to the New Monthly Magazine set up by Phillips the bookseller, and edited by Dr. Aikin. Accordingly we set off and proceeded along the Quantock Hills towards Watchet, and in the course of this walk was planned the Poem of The Ancient Mariner. . . . We began the composition together, on that, to me, memorable evening. . . . We returned after a few days from a delightful tour, of

[1] "My First Acquaintance with Poets", in *The Liberal* (1823).
[2] *Prelude*[1], xiii. 393.

which I have many pleasant, and some of them droll-enough, recollections. We returned by Dulverton to Alfoxden. The Ancient Mariner
grew and grew till it became too important for our first object, which
was limited to our expectation of five pounds, and we began to talk of a
Volume, which was to consist, as Mr. Coleridge has told the world, of
poems chiefly on natural subjects taken from common life, but looked
at, as much as might be, through an imaginative medium.

Wordsworth was fond of describing this walk. He spoke of
it earlier to Alexander Dyce, and later in 1844 to Mrs. Davy
and others, and in 1847 to his nephew and biographer
Christopher Wordsworth, but these accounts do not precisely date the walk, and add nothing material to the Fenwick
note.[1] This stands as I have given it, with the omission of
some passages on Wordsworth's own small contributions to
The Ancient Mariner, in the Moxon *Wordsworth* of 1857,
where first the Fenwick notes appeared in full.[2] But it had
already been used by Christopher Wordsworth in the
Memoirs (1851), and here the walk is dated, not "in the spring
of the year 1798" but in "the autumn of 1797".[3] The cor-
rection may, I suppose, have emerged in the course of
Christopher's own conversation with his uncle, although in
that, as recorded, the notice of the walk is immediately followed by a reference to poems which Wordsworth wrote "in
the course of that spring". Or it may be taken from the
Sibylline Leaves, or perhaps more probably from two letters
of Dorothy Wordsworth, which the biographer had just
quoted as follows:

In November, 1797, Wordsworth and his sister accompanied
Coleridge in a pedestrian tour along the sea-coast to Minehead, thence
to Porlock. "From Porlock" says Miss Wordsworth, "we kept close to
the shore about four miles. Our road lay through wood, rising almost
perpendicularly from the sea, with views of the opposite mountains of
Wales: thence we came by twilight to Lynmouth, in Devonshire.
The next morning we were guided to a valley at the top of one of those
immense hills which open at each end to the sea, and is from its rocky
appearance called the Valley of Stones. We mounted a cliff at the end
of the valley, and looked from it immediately on to the sea." They were

[1] Campbell, p. 594; *Wordsworth Memoirs*, i. 15; ii. 444.
[2] i. 181.   [3] i. 106.

struck by the wild grandeur of the scenery, and returned home gratified by the tour. On 20th November, Miss Wordsworth writes, "We have been on another tour: we set out last Monday evening [13th November] at half past four. The evening was dark and cloudy: we went eight miles, William and Coleridge employing themselves in laying the plan of a ballad, to be published with some pieces of William's".[1]

The date originally given in the Fenwick note to the Dulverton walk, even apart from its clash with Coleridge's own, cannot possibly, I think, be right. Dorothy's *Alfoxden Journal* and Coleridge's movements, as disclosed by his correspondence, leave no room for it between 20th January and 17th May, 1798. There was a walk to Lynton at least, with Cottle, at the end of May or early in June, but that is too late, as *The Ancient Mariner* was then ready for the press.

So much, for the moment, of *The Ancient Mariner*. The direct evidence as to the three other poems involved is, happily, shorter. For the First Part of *Christabel* we have the already quoted references of it in 1815 and 1825 to the same "year" as *The Ancient Mariner*, and a more precise statement in the preface to the first edition of 1816 that it was written in "the year one thousand seven hundred and ninety seven". This date Coleridge had already given in a letter of 22nd October, 1815, to Lord Byron, with the amplification:

> I should say that the plan of the whole poem was formed and the first Book and half of the second were finished—and it was not till after my return from Germany in the year 1800 that I resumed it—and finished the second and a part of the third book.[2]

There can be little doubt that the whole of the Second Part, as we know it, was written after the return from Germany, and there is no trace of any fragment of a Third Part. Moreover, as late as about 1820, he referred to the fragment as of two cantos.[3] He may have had a different plan for the distribution of the existing matter in 1815.

The Dark Ladie was being prepared, according to the *Biographia Literaria*, for the *Lyrical Ballads*, and cannot therefore be later than 1798. In 1802 Coleridge hoped soon to

---

[1] i. 105. [2] Griggs, ii. 146.
[3] T. Allsop, *Letters, Conversations and Recollections of S.T.C.*, (Ed. 2), 51.

send the completion of it to a lady, Miss Sotheby, who had
been pleased with "the first part".[1] The existing fragment
of 60 lines was printed, with asterisks to denote omissions, in
the *Poetical Works* of 1834. An undated list of poems in Coleridge's hand shows that there were once 190 lines. The last
three stanzas are found separately in a manuscript. They
tell of a wedding, with "nodding minstrels", and Professor
Lowes suggests that their substance may have been taken up
into *The Ancient Mariner*.[2] They are not, however, in the
same metrical form.

The Three Graves is also incomplete. Part III of 169 lines
and Part IV of 149 lines were printed in *The Friend* for 21st
September, 1809, as from a tale of six Parts, the two last
of which might be given thereafter. A prose sketch of the
story "as it is contained in the first and second parts" is
appended. Coleridge says that the verses were composed
"somewhat more than twelve years ago", which takes them
back at least to 1797; and they may be earlier still, as he adds
that he had been reading Bryan Edwards's account of *Oby*
witchcraft, which we know that he borrowed from the Bristol
Library on 14th July and returned on 7th August, 1795.[3]
Parts III and IV were reprinted in *Sibylline Leaves* (1817),
with substantially the same statement and a final note, "*Car-
men reliquum in futurum tempus relegatum. To-morrow!* and
To-morrow! and *To-morrow!*" There is an unfinished
manuscript draft of 219 lines, which clearly represents Parts
I and II, but nothing is known of Parts V and VI.

Dorothy Wordsworth, who records the planning of a ballad
in her letter of 20th November, 1797, records the end of one
in the journal which she kept at Alfoxden from 20th January
to 17th May, 1798.[4]

23rd [March.] Coleridge dined with us. He brought his ballad
finished. We walked with him to the Miner's house. A beautiful
evening, very starry, the horned moon.

[1] *Letters*, i. 375.   [2] Lowes, p. 577.
[3] Bryan Edwards, *History of the British Colonies in the West Indies* (1793),
vol. ii; *Modern Philology*, xxi. 317.
[4] W. Knight, *Journals of D. W.* (1897), i. 3–18.

It is perhaps reasonable to suppose that both records are of the same ballad, and, so far as time-indications go, this may also be the ballad of Coleridge's letters. That this should be "finished" on 18th February and "finished" again on 23rd March need not trouble us. Dorothy's ballad is generally taken to be *The Ancient Mariner* and its initiation put accordingly on 13th November, 1797. This is in many ways plausible. *The Ancient Mariner* has the "horned moon", which Dorothy had already noted in her journal on 21st March. Elsewhere, as Professor Lowes points out, she generally speaks of the "crescent moon".[1] And *The Ancient Mariner* was certainly planned on a walk. Moreover, the late start of Dorothy's letter looks like the late start of Wordsworth's narrative. There are, however, some difficulties to be faced. Dorothy's letters, quoted by Christopher Wordsworth and probably written to Mary Hutchinson, are unfortunately not preserved. So far as the extracts go, they describe not one walk but two, do not date the first, do not in either case refer to a long detour homewards by Dulverton, and do not give the direction of the second at all. Two walks as far as Dulverton, each at a cost to economical people of at least £5, are not very likely, but conceivably the walk recalled by Wordsworth might be either of them. If it was the first, the ballad of the second and probably also that of the journal would be other than *The Ancient Mariner*. I am inclined, however, to think that it was the second, for this reason. The scheme for *Cain* preceded that for *The Ancient Mariner*. But the scene of *Cain*, if Hazlitt may be trusted, was to have been the Valley of Rocks at Lynton, and Dorothy's reference to the use of a guide to the Valley on the earlier walk certainly suggests that it was Coleridge's own first visit to that wild place. *Cain* was abandoned for *The Ancient Mariner*, and the second walk would fit in well enough for that. There is, however, a discrepancy to be noted between Dorothy's account and Wordsworth's. She says that the ballad of 13th November was to be published with some pieces of Wordsworth's, which is what in fact happened to *The Ancient Mariner*; he that *The Ancient Mariner* was to be

[1] Lowes, p. 184.

sold for £5 to Phillips. This also was Coleridge's intention
for the ballad of his letters, on 6th January, 1798. By 18th
February he had diverted it to a volume, not of Wordsworth's,
but of his own. Dorothy's statement, being contemporary,
must of course be accepted. Possibly Wordsworth's memory
had confused a second intention with a first, which also became a fourth. But if the ballad of 13th November is also the
ballad of Coleridge's letters, there is yet another question to
be put. No doubt *The Ancient Mariner* "grew and grew".
But can we believe that a poem which was finished by 18th
February in 340 lines, and finished again by 23rd March,
grew into a poem of 658 lines before it was printed in June?
If so, an entire revolution in scale and scope was entailed. I
do not like to suggest that Coleridge may have originally
written in "fourteeners"; his models, in Percy's *Reliques*,
would not put him on that track. Part I of *Christabel* comes
nearer to the measure of 340 lines; it has 265 as first printed,
257 and 266 in two manuscripts; its *Conclusion*, if that is of
the same date, adds another 53. But Coleridge can
never have supposed that *Christabel* was "finished". *The
Dark Ladie* is clearly too short. Parts III and IV of *The Three
Graves* come to 318, which is fairly near.

I am afraid that the problem of identity between ballad
and ballad is hardly soluble with certainty on these lines.
There is some further evidence, both for *The Ancient Mariner*
and for *Christabel*, although the name of neither poem occurs
in it. I have noted the appearance of the "horned moon" in
Dorothy Wordsworth's *Alfoxden Journal*. This yields further
parallels of phrase to the poems. I give them as others have
given them, but listed in order of time:

(1) *21st January.* Those oaks, fanned by the sea breeze, thick with
feathery sea-green moss, as a grove not stripped of its leaves; *17th
February.* The bright green moss was bare at the roots of the trees.
A.M. 552.   He kneels at morn and noon and eve—
                     He hath a cushion plump:
                     It is the moss, that wholly hides
                     The rotted old Oak-stump.
Chr. 33.   And naught was green upon the oak
                     But moss and rarest misletoe.

280 (*Conclusion*).   She
    Was praying at the old oak tree.
    Amid the jaggèd shadows
    Of mossy leafless boughs.

(2) *25th January*. The sky spread over with one continuous cloud, whitened by the light of the moon. . . . At once the clouds seemed to cleave asunder, and left her in the centre of a black-blue vault.
 A.M. 314. Hark! hark! the thick black cloud is cleft,
     And the Moon is at its side.

(3) *27th January*. The manufacturer's dog makes a strange, uncouth howl.
 Chr. 11.   Ever and aye, by shine and shower,
     Sixteen short howls, not over loud.

(4) *31st January*. The moon immensely large, the sky scattered over with clouds. These soon closed in, contracting the dimensions of the moon without concealing her.
 Chr. 16.   The thin gray cloud is spread on high,
     It covers but not hides the sky.
     The moon is behind, and at the full;
     And yet she looks both small and dull.

(5) *8th February*. Sat a considerable time upon the heath. Its surface restless and glittering with the motion of the scattered piles of withered grass, and the waving of the spiders' threads.
 A.M. 175. Are those *her* Sails that glance in the Sun
     Like restless gossameres?

(6) *17th February*. The branches of the hollies pendent with their white burden. . . . The bare branches of the oaks thickened by the snow.
 A.M. 568. When the Ivy-tod is heavy with snow.

(7) *7th March*. Only one leaf upon the top of a tree—the sole remaining leaf—danced round and round like a rag blown by the wind.
 Chr. 48. There is not wind enough to twirl
     The one red leaf, the last of its clan,
     That dances as often as dance it can,
     Hanging so light, and hanging so high,
     On the topmost twig that looks up at the sky.

(8) *21st March*. Startled two night birds from the great elm tree.
 A.M. 569. And the Owlet whoops to the wolf below.

Chr. 2.   And the owls have awakened the crowing cock;
Tu-whit!—Tu-whoo!

306 (*Conclusion*).   By tairn and rill
The night-birds all that hour were still.
But now they are jubilant anew,
From cliff and tower, tu-whoo! tu-whoo!
Tu-whoo! tu-whoo! from wood and fell!

(9) *20th March.* The spring seemingly very little advanced; *24th March.* The spring continues to advance very slowly; *6th April.* The Spring still advancing very slowly; *12th April.* The Spring advances rapidly.

Chr. 21.   'Tis a month before the month of May,
And the Spring comes slowly up this way.

(10) *24th March.* A duller night than last night. . . . The stars dim.

A.M. (1800, *not* 1798) 206.
The stars were dim, and thick the night.

(11) *24th March.* Nothing green but the brambles that still retain their old leaves, the evergreens and the palms. . . . The crooked arm of the old oak tree points upwards to the moon.

Chr. 33.   And naught was green upon the oak
But moss and rarest misletoe:
She kneels beneath the huge oak tree.

(12) *25th March.* The night cloudy but not dark.

Chr. 14.   Is the night chilly and dark?
The night is chilly, but not dark.

Individually these parallels, except perhaps No. 7, are trivial; notes of recurrent natural phenomena, which both friends may have often observed, and may have observed together. Taken in mass they do at least suggest that the same images were present to the mind of Dorothy when she made the entries in her *Journal* and to that of Coleridge when he worked on *The Ancient Mariner* and *Christabel*; or, more precisely, on passages of *Christabel*, since the parallels are concentrated in the first fifty-two lines and the *Conclusion*. E. H. Coleridge went further, and asserted that the observations "were jotted down by Dorothy, and, then or afterwards, found their way into Coleridge's verse". This seems to have been his main reason, when he published his fine edition of *Christabel* in

1907, for rejecting Coleridge's own date of 1797 as that of Part I and substituting 1798. But Professor Lowes has pointed out, on the analogy of Dorothy's habit in later years, that any transference may just as well have been the other way, through the setting down in the *Journal* of phrases heard from poems read by Coleridge which clung to Dorothy's memory, and were revived by the sight of the objects portrayed. Thus in 1802, long after the publication of *The Ancient Mariner*, she wrote: "The moon came out suddenly ... and a star or two besides."¹ Professor Lowes does not, however, think that this can account for all the parallels with *Christabel*. And indeed there may be some temporal significance in the double reference to the late spring, which fits the facts of April, 1798. E. H. Coleridge also thought that Coleridge could not have written *Christabel* in 1797, because he was busy with *Osorio*, and was not likely to begin it before he had finished *The Ancient Mariner*, and he notes from *The Prelude* that *Christabel* was being chanted to the Quantock combes in the summer of 1798. But *Osorio* was over by October, 1797, and anyway Coleridge was not the man to be deterred from starting upon one thing by the mere fact that he ought to have been winding up another. And in the summer of 1798 he was admittedly working on the continuation of *Christabel*. Moreover, Wordsworth himself was chanting *The Thorn*, which he had written on 19th March. E. H Coleridge does not explain why he reverted to 1797 for Part I in his full edition of the *Poems* in 1912. At one time he seems to have put it between 23rd March and 14th May, 1798, for he noted "The *Poem* as I suppose *Christabel*" on his transcript of a letter of the latter date from the poet to his brother George, in which he says:

I have written a Poem lately which I think even the Major [James Coleridge] (who is no admirer of the art) would like.²

There is, however, little in *Christabel* to appeal to the imagination of a Major of Volunteers, and surely this poem was *Fears in Solitude*, written on 20th April, 1798, just after a visit to Ottery, and in a scare of invasion.

¹ Lowes, pp. 175, 179, 512.   ² Griggs, i. 105.

Finally there is the famous *Gutch Note Book*, with the help of which Professor Lowes has traced so much of the omnivorous reading that welled up in *The Ancient Mariner*.[1] This reading goes back at least to 1795, but *The Ancient Mariner* seems to have fallen inheritor to several earlier schemes, which never came to fruition. One was the "Wandering Jew, a romance", the title of which Coleridge jotted down in 1795. *Cain*, perhaps an outgrowth from this, was another. A third was a series of hymns on the sun and moon, and probably the elements, already known of by Charles Lamb in June, 1796.[2] A fourth was a play of *Siberian Exiles*, which had been in Coleridge's mind shortly before January, 1798. Professor Lowes thinks also that a bassoon hoped for by the Stowey choir in 1797 may be the bassoon of *The Ancient Mariner*.[3] All this fits in well enough with Coleridge's own date for that poem. The traces of *Christabel* in the *Note Book* are slighter. Many of its entries cannot be chronologically fixed. It was certainly in use from 1795 until well into 1798. A note, not in Coleridge's own hand, on the last page, of the distance from a "passage" to Abergavenny, suggests his visit to John Thelwall at Llyswen, beyond Abergavenny, in the August of that year. But I think that the book falls into two sections. The first half of it seems to have been filled up continuously from 1795 to late 1797 or 1798.[4] Near the end of this is recorded a childish incident of Hartley Coleridge.

Hartley fell down and hurt himself—I caught him up crying and screaming—and ran out of room with him.—The Moon caught his eye—he ceased crying immediately—and his eyes and the tears in them, how they glittered in the Moonlight![5]

Hartley, born on 19th September, 1796, cannot well have been old enough to fall and hurt himself before the autumn of 1797, and the entry may be later still. The second half of the book is broken by blank pages here and there, and seems to consist of casual memoranda, set down at various dates.[6] They cannot form part of a chronological series with the first

---

[1] B.M. Add. MS. 27901, printed, not very accurately, in *Archiv f. neueren Sprachen und Litteraturen*, xcvii (1896), 333, by A. Brandl.

[2] *Letters* (ed. Lucas), i. 27, 92.   [3] Lowes, p. 213.

[4] ff. 2–37.   [5] f. 32.   [6] ff. 38^v–89^v.

half, since some of them almost certainly go back to events of 1795 and 1796.

Hartley's adventure fused itself in Coleridge's mind with two other thoughts, which are also in the *Note Book*. Here he had written, as far back as 1796:

> Discontent
> Mild as an Infant low-plaining in its sleep;

then some references on Plato's myth of the Cave, and then another comment:

> In a distempered dream things and forms in themselves common and harmless inflict a terror of anguish.[1]

And so we get in *The Nightingale* of April, 1798:

> He knows well
> The evening-star; and once, when he awoke
> In most distressful mood (some inward pain
> Had made up that strange thing, an infant's dream—)
> I hurried with him to our orchard-plot,
> And he beheld the moon, and, hushed at once,
> Suspends his sobs, and laughs most silently,
> While his fair eyes, that swam with undropped tears,
> Did glitter in the yellow moon-beam!

This, in turn, has been compared with lines in the *Conclusion* to Part I of *Christabel*.

> And see! the lady Christabel
> Gathers herself from out her trance;
> Her limbs relax, her countenance
> Grows sad and soft; the smooth thin lids
> Close o'er her eyes; and tears she sheds—
> Large tears that leave the lashes bright!
> And oft the while she seems to smile
> As infants at a sudden light!

A doubt arises, through E. H. Coleridge's suggestion that, whatever the date of Part I itself, the *Conclusion* belongs to 1800. There does not seem to be much basis for this, beyond the use of the northern words "fell" and "tairn", which may well have been learnt from the Wordsworths as early as 1797.

[1] ff. 28ᵛ, 29.

One other entry in the *Note Book* clearly found its way into
Christabel.

> Behind the thin
> Gray cloud that cover'd but not hid the sky
> The round full moon look'd small.[1]

This comes just before Hartley, and may therefore be of
either 1797 or 1798. It is nearer than Dorothy's *Journal* to
Coleridge's.

> The thin gray cloud is spread on high,
> It covers but not hides the sky.
> The moon is behind, and at the full;
> And yet she looks both small and dull.

It must be added that the *Note Book* jottings were not always,
although they often were, used in poems of more or less even
date. Sometimes, like the Platonic notes of 1796, they were
referred to, or floated back into Coleridge's memory, after an
interval. One is in *Love*, which can hardly have been written
before the first meeting with Sara Hutchinson in October,
1799; another perhaps in *The Picture*, not otherwise traceable
before 1802.[2] There is a "daimonic" element in *Christabel*,
but this was an old preoccupation of Coleridge, even before
his acquisition of Psellus, *De Daemonibus*, in November,
1796.[3]

If I may register a resultant personal impression, where
the evidence is at once so copious and so inconclusive, it
must be, apart from the question of the identity of ballad with
ballad, which eludes us, that *The Ancient Mariner* and
Christabel largely proceeded *pari passu*; that the initiation of
The Ancient Mariner was probably the earlier; and that, while
there is no sufficient ground for substantially rejecting
Coleridge's own ascription of Part I of *Christabel* to 1797,
touches may well have been added to its opening and perhaps the *Conclusion* written in the spring of 1798. It would
be a natural evolution from the rather crude balladry of *The
Three Graves* to *The Ancient Mariner*, still in strict ballad
form, and from that to the more free rhythmic handling of

---

[1] f. 31.   [2] ff. 31, 36ᵛ.
[3] *Letters*, i. 182; cf. Lowes, pp. 229

ballad-themes in *Christabel*, and in the stanza, not itself a ballad-stanza, of *The Dark Ladie.*

The date of *Kubla Khan* is a problem by itself. For this, too, there are hints in the *Note Book*. The poem has its "demon-lover". In 1796 Coleridge set down "a river run under ground" as an image for the re-emergence of old opinions. A note from Thomas Maurice's *History of Hindostan* (1795), of an image of ice in a cave of Cashmere is undatable.[1] The account of Hartley's fall is framed in extracts from William Bartram's *Travels* (1791), which Coleridge was evidently reading on that night. It gave him his first note after the interruption:

Some wilderness-plot, green and fountainous and unviolated by Man.[2]

And the influence of this Professor Lowes traces both in the scenery of *Kubla Khan* and in a letter of March, 1798, to George Coleridge on the "divine repose" of laudanum.[3] We may safely put Coleridge's knowledge of Bartram's book as early as 1797. It contributed to *Cain*, as well as to *The Ancient Mariner*. It may have influenced a passage of *Osorio.* In a note of 1800 to *The Lime-Tree Bower*, written early in July, 1797, Coleridge says that "some months after" he found a parallel to one of its lines in Bartram. But I doubt whether Professor Lowes is justified in an inference that he had already read the *Travels* in 1794 or early in 1795.[4] This rests on an early draft of *Lewti*, the "Tamaha" of which is an adaptation of Bartram's "Alatamaha". In this draft the object of the poem is not a Lewti but a Mary. Professor Lowes, however, himself cites a statement by Southey that it was a boyish poem of Wordsworth's, corrected by Coleridge. There seems no reason for rejecting this, and we may suspect that Mary was not Mary Evans, but Mary Hutchinson. Certainly Wordsworth, as well as Coleridge, knew and used Bartram.

When Coleridge published *Kubla Khan* in 1816, he wrote

In the summer of the year 1797, the Author, then in ill health,

[1] ff. 26ᵛ, 45ᵛ. [2] f. 32.
[3] *Letters* i. 239, but there postdated; cf. Lowes, p. 364.
[4] Lowes, p. 513.

had retired to a lonely farm-house between Porlock and Linton, on the Exmoor confines of Somerset and Devonshire. In consequence of a light indisposition, an anodyne had been prescribed.

It was under the influence of this that he composed the poem in his sleep. In 1893 Campbell transferred it from 1797 to 1798 and related it to a "rupture" with Charles Lloyd, and gave his justification as follows:

A MS. note by Coleridge, dated Nov. 3, 1810, has been discovered, in which it is stated that the retirement to the farm-house, and the recourse to opium—he calls it "the first", meaning, doubtless, the first recourse for relief from *mental* trouble—were caused by the breach with Lloyd. He goes on to say that the nervous disquietude and misery which he suffered prevented him from finishing *Christabel*.[1]

The discovery was made by E. H. Coleridge, who wrote in 1895—

The MS. note of November 10, 1810, to which a previous reference has been made, connects a serious quarrel with Lloyd, and consequent distress of mind, with the retirement to "the lonely farmhouse" and a first recourse to opium. If, as the letters intimate, these events must be assigned to May, 1798, it follows that "Kubla Khan" was written at the same time.[2]

I cannot find any "previous reference", but in the *Poems* of 1912 E. H. Coleridge puts *Kubla Khan* under 1798 and says—

There can be little doubt that Coleridge should have written "the summer of 1798". In an unpublished MS. note, dated November 3, 1810, he connects the retirement between "Linton and Porlock" and a recourse to opium with his quarrel with Charles Lloyd, and consequent distress of mind. That quarrel was at its height in May, 1798.

I have been particular about these accounts, because the variant terminology of "rupture", "breach", and "quarrel" suggests that we have nothing more than paraphrases of the note. It is still unpublished, and the Rev. G. H. B. Coleridge, who was kind enough to make a search for me, tells me that he cannot see it in his father's transcript of the poet's notebook for 1810. Possibly it may have gone astray with other material for E. H. Coleridge's projected *Life*.[3]

[1] *Poems* (1893), xlii.   [2] *Letters*, i. 245.   [3] Cf. Griggs, i. xii.

There were two occasions, one in 1797 and one in 1798, on which Coleridge's relations with Charles Lloyd caused him acute distress.. Lloyd had visited him at Bristol in the autumn of 1796, and had been attacked there with epileptic fits. An arrangement was made for their domicile together at Stowey. During the move, Lloyd went home to Birmingham, and thence to London, where he became very friendly with Charles Lamb. He reached Stowey early in February, 1797, stayed for a fortnight with Thomas Poole, and took up his quarters in Coleridge's cottage on 22nd February.[1] He brought with him poems, which he gave to Coleridge for publication with his own and Lamb's.[2] They were printed by July and published in October.[3] A fortnight after his arrival at the cottage, the fits recurred in a serious form. Coleridge was still nursing him on 16th March, but shortly afterwards he went home.[4] There is no clear sign of a "rupture" or "breach" or "quarrel" at this time, although anything, I suppose, might happen between a sensitive and poverty-stricken poet and an epilept. Certainly Coleridge was much perturbed. He wrote to Cottle:

When last in Bristol the day I meant to have devoted to you was such a day of sadness, that I could *do nothing.*—On the Saturday, the Sunday, and the ten days after my arrival at Stowey I felt a depression too dreadful to be described. . . . Wordsworth's conversation, etc., roused me somewhat; but even now I am not the man I have been— and I think never shall. A sort of calm hopelessness diffuses itself over my heart. Indeed every mode of life which has promised me bread and cheese, has been, one after another torn away from me—but God remains. I have no immediate pressing distress, having received ten pounds from Lloyd's father at Birmingham.[5]

There is nothing here which necessarily points to anything but financial embarrassment. Coleridge had doubtless planned his Stowey expenses on the basis of a contribution from Lloyd, although to what extent is not clear, in view of

---

[1] E. V. Lucas, *Charles Lamb and the Lloyds*, p. 37.
[2] *E. R.* i. 232; *Rem.* p. 132.
[3] Harvard 19478. 5. F; *Monthly Magazine*, iv. 304.
[4] *E. R.* i. 197; *Rem.* p. 107; Griggs, i. 72; Greever, p. 29; Lamb, i. 98.
[5] Griggs, i. 70.

the shifting negotiations with Lloyd's father in 1796. The
letter to Cottle is undated, but Coleridge's name was entered
for a book at the Bristol Library on 23rd March and he took
it away a fortnight later.[1] Incidentally it seems clear that
Wordsworth, who left Racedown for a fortnight in Bristol on
19th March, was with him at Stowey in April.[2] Our knowledge of Coleridge's further movements up to June is scrappy.
There was at least one other visit to Bristol, where the joint
Poems were being printed. There is room for a retirement
to the farm-house near Porlock in the latter part of April or
May, and perhaps between 16th and 23rd March. But there
is no evidence of illness, other than mental, during this
spring.

On 5th June Poole invited Lloyd to contribute to a fund
for Coleridge, which shows that he at least was aware of no
ill feeling.[3] About 20th September Lamb wrote to Coleridge,
"You use Lloyd very ill, never writing to him".[4] A failure
to write does not, with Coleridge, imply estrangement.
There had, however, been at least one letter, enclosing a copy
of the July *Lime Bower* poem.[5] It has not been printed, and
I do not know where it is. Meanwhile Lloyd, improved in
health, had fallen in love with Sophia Pemberton. There was
family opposition. He came to Lamb in trouble about 10th
August, and carried him off on a visit to Southey at Burton
in Hampshire. He had thought of consulting Coleridge, but
said that "if he *had* come to you, he could never have brought
himself to leave you". Here again is no sign of ill will. Lamb
left Lloyd at Burton after one night's stay, and then Lloyd
and Southey went together to Bath and on to Birmingham,
for the purpose of persuading Sophia to a Scotch marriage.[6]
According to De Quincey, Southey stole her away for Lloyd
"by proxy".[7] That is absurd; Lloyd and Sophia were not
married until 1799. Evidently the attempt was abandoned,

[1] *Modern Philology*, xxi. 317; *E. R.* i. 211; *Rem.* p. 117.
[2] *W. F. L.* i. 104, misdated 1796.
[3] Sandford, *Thomas Poole and his Friends* (1888), i. 228.
[4] Lamb, i. 112.
[5] *Poems* (1893), p. 591.   [6] Lamb, i. 109.
[7] *Tait's Magazine* (March 1840).

and by 3rd September Lloyd had returned with Southey to Burton. Southey's own letters about his relations with Lloyd are curiously cryptic.[1] On 3rd September he writes to Grosvenor Bedford:

It is a huge while since I have written to you. I have been an immensity of way since—even to the middle of Warwickshire, the quares why & the propter becauses of which, must be learnt hereafter. The result is that Charles Lloyd is with us at Burton.

And on 16th September, now from Bath—

Charles Lloyd is still my companion. I never expected [to ha]ve another friend, & yet chance has birdlimed me to one in the most odd manner.

And on 19th November—

Charles Lloyd is coming to London with me—& means to lodge in the same house. How all this chanced is a long & odd story. I could wish you to know him well—but it would be an effort to give his character—& I love not exertion. Thus much however I will say—his feelings are too susceptible of neglect or kindness, they are not so blunt as we could wish them—or as they should be for his own happiness, & a little attention to him in conversation—& any trifling mark of kindness will highly gratify him.

On 11th November he wrote to his brother Tom that Lloyd had written a novel, which was no doubt *Edmund Oliver*.[2] Lloyd did not lodge long with Southey in London, but joined James White, and the constant society of the pair became a source of some irritation to Lamb, who was absorbed in his sister's state of health.[3] So he wrote to Coleridge on 28th January, and so too, probably, implies in his *Old Familiar Faces*. For some of what follows we are dependent on an undated letter from Coleridge to Lamb during the summer of 1798.[4] Coleridge's Nehemiah Higginbottom sonnets had appeared in December, 1797. They do not seem to have perturbed Lamb on his own account; he makes no reference to them on 28th January. But they did perturb Southey,

---

[1] Bodl. MS. Eng. Letters, c. 23, ff. 15, 20, 28^v.
[2] *Letters* (ed. Warter), i. 46.   [3] Lamb, i. 114.
[4] *Letters*, i. 249.

who thought that he was one of the poets aimed at. Coleridge denied this to him on 8th December, 1797.[1] But Lamb, for some reason, discredited the denial. According to Coleridge—

When I wrote to you that my Sonnet to Simplicity was not composed with reference to Southey, you answered me (I believe these were the words): "It was a lie too gross for the grossest ignorance to believe"; and I was not angry with you, because the assertion which the grossest ignorance would believe a lie the Omniscient knew to be truth.[2]

That it was truth, we are assured by Coleridge's letter to Cottle in November, 1797. On 8th March, 1798, Coleridge, then planning a third edition of his *Poems*, had been informed by Cottle that Lloyd wished his to be omitted. He agreed, with the comment, "By past experiences we build up our moral being".[3] Two undated letters evidently followed.[4] In one he tells Cottle that he is "willing to believe myself in part mistaken" and has no wish for or against the republication of the poems; in the other that he never involved Cottle in the bickering.

Your letter supplied only one in a link of circumstances, that informed me of some things, and perhaps deceived me in others. I shall write to-day to Lloyd.

There was certainly some correspondence with Lloyd, and either before or in the middle of it Coleridge must have seen *Edmund Oliver*, which was dedicated to Lamb, and published by Cottle in April, 1798.[5] This was a gross attack upon Coleridge. The imaginary hero is given his personal appearance, his "large glistening eye" and "dark hair", and to him is ascribed, not only Coleridge's adventure in the army, after a love-affair which was not quite the same, but even, in more than one place, his addiction to opium. It was a bombshell to Coleridge. To Estlin he wrote on 14th May—

I have had many sorrows and some that bite deep; calumny and ingratitude from men who have been fostered in the bosom of my confidence![6]

[1] *Letters*, i. 251. [2] *Letters*, i. 249.
[3] *E. R.* i. 294; *Rem.* p. 164. [4] *E. R.* i. 297, 300; *Rem.* pp. 165, 167.
[5] *Monthly Magazine*, v. 297. [6] *Letters*, i. 246.

And to Poole on the same day—

I have had lately some sorrows that have cut more deeply into my heart than they ought to have done.[1]

On 16th May he set out on a walk with Wordsworth and Dorothy to Bridgewater, Cheddar, and Cross, and of this he tells Estlin that Wordsworth's "main business was to bring back poor Lloyd, whose infirmities have been made the instruments of another man's darker passions". They had learnt on the way that Lloyd had gone to Birmingham, but Wordsworth had proceeded to Bristol to make sure.[2] On 20th May he writes again to Poole:

So many unpleasant and shocking circumstances have happened to me in my immediate knowledge within the last fortnight, that I am in a nervous state, and the most trifling thing makes we weep.[3]

There can be little doubt that the other man of Coleridge's suspicions was Southey, with whom his reconciliation after their quarrel in 1795 had never been whole-hearted; and little doubt also, I am afraid, that those suspicions were justified. We have seen that *Edmund Oliver* was being written in Southey's house at Burton; and that Southey suggested it, or at least provided material for it, seems a natural inference from the fact that "my novel, in three volumes, of Edmund Oliver" appears in a list of projected works which he sent to Grosvenor Bedford on 31st July, 1796.[4] Having given away the name, however, he did not altogether drop the design. His commonplace book of 1798 or 1799 contemplates a novel with an army hero, under the title of *Oliver Elton*, and in 1801 he added a note to omit "the soldier part".[5] How far Coleridge ever learnt all about the genesis of *Edmund Oliver* must remain uncertain. In August, 1799, when making a move for a renewed reconciliation with Southey, he says that he never charged him with anything but "deep and implacable enmity" towards himself;[6] and in

---

[1] *Letters*, i. 248.
[2] *Letters*, i. 245; *Alfoxden Journal* (22nd May in error for 17th May).
[3] *Letters*, i. 249.   [4] *Life and Correspondence*, i. 286.
[5] Ed. J. W. Warter, iv. 9.   [6] Griggs, i. 123.

October, after the reconciliation had been effected, he says of
Edmund Oliver—

You remember Lloyd's own account of this story, of course, more
accurately than I, and can, therefore, best judge how far my suspicions
of falsehood and exaggeration were well-founded.[1]

Just before, or soon after, the attempt to recover Lloyd at
Bristol must come Coleridge's undated letter to Lamb.[2] He
has been told by Lloyd through Dorothy Wordsworth that
Lamb no longer intends to correspond with him. For that
he feels no resentment; Lamb has misunderstood him. From
Lloyd he has had letters for which he wishes the writer may
feel remorse. Lamb had disbelieved him about the sonnets,
when he spoke the truth.

This, however, makes me cautious not too hastily to affirm the falsehood of an assertion of Lloyd's that in Edmund Oliver's love-fit, leaving
college, and going into the army he had no sort of allusion to or recollection of my love-fit, leaving college, and going into the army, and
that he never thought of my person in the description of Oliver's person
in the first letter of the second volume.

And now—

I write to you not that I wish to hear from you, but that I wish
you to write to Lloyd and press upon him the propriety, nay the necessity,
of his giving me a meeting either *tête-à-tête* or in the presence of all
whose esteem I value. This I owe to my own character; I owe it to
him if by any means he may even yet be extricated. He assigned as
reasons for his rupture my vices; and he is either right or wrong. If
right, it is fit that others should know it and follow his example; if
wrong, he has acted very wrong.

This is the only thing which suggests a possible "rupture" in
March, 1797, since Lloyd cannot have had any personal
experience of Coleridge's "vices" since that date. We do not
know what reply, if any, Lamb made. In June Cottle wrote
to Lloyd, urging a visit of reconciliation to Coleridge, and
Lloyd excused himself.

I cannot think that I have acted with, or from, passion towards him.
Even my solitary night thoughts have been easy and calm when they
have dwelt on him. . . . I love Coleridge, and can forget all that has

---

[1] *Letters*, i. 311.   [2] *Letters*, i. 249.

happened. At present I could not well go to Stowey. I could scarcely excuse so sudden a removal from my parents. . . . I shall write to Coleridge to-day.[1]

All very well, but of course the only unforgettable thing was *Edmund Oliver*, a very different affair from the legitimate, if unwise, literary criticism of the Higginbottom sonnets. So ends the story, so far as Charles Lloyd is concerned. The friction between Coleridge and Lamb lasted until Coleridge left for Germany, but I need not go into the later stages of that. Let Lamb's reminiscence of 1832 be its epitaph.

If you ever thought an offence, much more wrote it, against me, it must have been in the times of Noah; and the great waters swept it away.[2]

On the whole I am disposed, in the absence of the note on *Kubla Khan*, to think with Campbell and E. H. Coleridge, that May, 1798, is the most likely date for the composition of that poem. Coleridge had been ill in March. The *Alfoxden Journal* shows him at Stowey from 6th to 8th May, and on 19th May he preached at Taunton. But on 9th May Dorothy wrote to him, which suggests an absence. Was it the letter which notified Lamb's secession? Anyhow, a retirement to the farm-house on 9th May would fit in very well with the fortnight's trouble of which Coleridge told Poole on 20th May. It might have been later in May than that letter. During most of June, first Cottle and then Hazlitt seem to have been visiting at Stowey. There was a walk to Lynton with each of them, but certainly no stop between that and Porlock on the second occasion, and probably none on the first.[3] Moreover, even if Coleridge did not read Bartram's *Travels* for the first time in the latter part of 1797, it was then or early in 1798 that he took the scenic hint which emerged in *Kubla Khan*.

1933.

ADDENDUM

I CAN now add something to my foregoing discussion of the date of *Kubla Khan*. I was there unable to trace a relevant note by Coleridge that had been used but not printed by E. H.

[1] Lucas, p. 54.   [2] Lamb, ii. 946; cf. i. 565.
[3] *E. R.* i. 311, 315; *Rem.* pp. 176, 179; Hazlitt, in *The Liberal* (1823).

Coleridge and J. D. Campbell. Later, the original notebook in which it occurs was found by the Rev. G. H. B. Coleridge, who very kindly sent it to me with leave to print the extract. Under the heading "Egoana" and the date "Saturday, Nov. 3, 1810, Hudson's Hotel, Covent Garden", the poet made a long entry, in which he laments that, although he has for fourteen years felt the most consummate friendship for a man, and for ten years has loved a woman, he has never himself been really loved, but has confounded being loved by a person with "a person's being highly pleased with being loved and admired by me". The references to Wordsworth and Sara Hutchinson are unmistakable. This passage has already been printed by T. M. Raysor in *Studies in Philology*, xxvi (1929), 321. His text has a good many variants of no great importance, but he worked from a transcript, and could not find the original. Then comes in the notebook a second passage, the writing of which suggests another sitting or the use of another pen. It is as follows:

Elucidation.

If ever there was a time and circumstance in my life in which I behaved *perfectly* well, it was in that of C. Lloyd's mad quarrel & frantic ingratitude to me —— He even wrote a letter to D. W., in which he not only called me a villain, but appealed to a conversation which passed between him & *her*, as the grounds of it—and as proving that this was her opinion no less than his—— She brought over the *letter* to me from Alfoxden with tears—— I laughed at it—— After this there succeeded, on his side a series of wicked calumnies & irritations—infamous Lies to Southey & to poor dear Lamb—in short, a conduct which was not that of a fiend, only because it was that of a madman—— on my side, patience, gentleness, and good for evil—yet this supernatural effort injured me——what I did not suffer to act on my mind, preyed on my body——it prevented my finishing the Christabel—& at the retirement between Linton & Porlock was the first occasion of my having recourse to Opium—— And all this was as well known to W & D W. as to myself—— Well! he settled in the North—& I determined to leave all my friends & follow him—— Soon after came —— Lloyd & settled at Ambleside——a thick acquaintance commenced between him and the W—— so that the fear of *his* coming in & receiving an unpleasant agitation occasioned such Looks & Hurry & Flurry & anxiety that I should be gone from Grasmere, as gave me

many a heart ache—— It was at this time that speaking of C.Ll.'s conduct to me & others I called him a rascal—— *D W* fired up, & said,
He was no rascal—in short, acted with at least as great warmth on
his behalf, as she ever could have done on mine—even when she had
known me to have acted the most nobly—— At length, a sort of reconciliation took place between me & C. Ll—— —— and about six or 8
months after, some person told *D. W.* that C. Ll. in a public Company
had given it as his opinion, that *Coleridge* was a greater poet, & possessed
of more genius by nature, than *W. W.* Instantly, D. W. pronounced
him a Villain. And thenceforward not a good word in his favor!!——

This passage cannot have been written much later than
that which preceded it. Together, they break in the middle
of a sentence some Shakespearean matter, of which part at
least was used in the lectures of 1811. The bitter tone of the
references to the Wordsworths must, of course, be dis-
counted. Coleridge was writing under the shock of the in-
discreet revelation by Basil Montagu of the warning given
by Wordsworth as to his domestic habits. He had no doubt
sought a temporary refuge in Hudson's Hotel after leaving
Montagu's house and before he went to the Morgans. I
am not, however, now concerned with that, but with the
bearing of the entry on the date of *Kubla Khan*. It makes no
mention of the poem, although it does of the farmhouse, and
of the recourse to opium. And now has appeared Lord
Crewe's holograph of what may be an early version of the
text, with a note which, like that printed in 1816, puts the
composition in 1797, but in the "fall", not the "summer".
So far as our scanty knowledge of Coleridge's movements in
September and October, 1797, goes, a retirement to the
farmhouse then is quite possible. It is conceivable, but not
I think likely, that he has confused two retirements.
He was fond of the Porlock district. In any case,
I do not think that the retirement of the notebook entry
can be placed earlier than the summer of 1798. It is linked
with the failure to finish *Christabel*. That does not take us
very far, since the chronology of *Christabel* is itself uncertain,
although the consonances with Dorothy Wordsworth's diary
make it on the whole probable that it was still in progress
during the spring of 1798. More conclusive is the mention

of a conversation about Coleridge between Dorothy and Charles Lloyd. There must at any rate have been the possibility of such a conversation. But Dorothy never saw Coleridge before June, 1797, and when she went to Stowey at the end of that month Lloyd was already gone. There is no evidence that he ever returned. He thought of doing so in August, but did not. The conversation is likely to have taken place during the December visit of the Wordsworth's to London, whither Lloyd had accompanied Southey. I daresay that Dorothy said that Coleridge was a villain about not answering letters, or something of that sort, and that Lloyd took it, or pretended to take it seriously. But the date of *Kubla Khan* is still a mystery.

1935.

MEREDITH'S "MODERN LOVE"

AMID THE "multitudinous chattering" of little singers, it not rarely happens that the authentic voice of poetic inspiration is unheard or disregarded. It has been Mr. Meredith's fortune to do greatly, not in one alone, but in two branches of creative literature, and in both to find his achievement unappreciated and his genius unacknowledged. But with this difference—that, whereas his prose at last enjoys an Indian summer of esteem, his verse, in itself no less admirable, is still left to wither in the eager airs of neglect. The critics have learnt to bow to the creator of Willoughby Patterne and Roy Richmond; but this newborn reverence has not been extended to the author of *Melampus* and *The Nuptials of Attila*. These, with their magnificent fellows, are still left as of old to be the refreshment and delight of "an acute and honourable minority".

We are supposed to be on the look-out for a laureate. I have certainly no desire to put a candidate in the field against Mr. William Watson and Mr. Lewis Morris. A garland that has been hawked about the streets is no meed for any poet to prize. But if, as one may think right, nationalism should be the note of a national bard, then there is not any other lyre which has sounded this note so long or so strenuously as this of Mr. Meredith. A passion of enthusiasm for the finer elements is Celt and Saxon and Norman; an irony-whetted insight into whatever of stupid or merely insular clogs these from aspiring: surely here are better qualities for our chosen singer than any gift of undiscriminating rhetoric or florid eulogy. It is the counsellor, the sage, that England has need of, not the panegyrist.

Yet how shall one recommend Mr. Meredith as a laureate to those who do not even know him as a poet? And it is to be feared that such is the parlous state of many who are familiar enough with *Richard Feverel* and *Emilia in England*. The revelation should not indeed come altogether as a surprise to such. Passage after passage in those most wonderful of romances is fulfilled with the lyric ecstasy. Think of the meeting of Richard and Lucy between the brambles and the water-lilies; think of the love-dream of Sandra Belloni beside the incantations of Wilming Weir:—

"The moon had now topped the cedar and was pure silver; silver on the grass, on the leafage, on the waters. And in the west, facing it, was an arch of twilight and tremulous rose; as if a spirit hung there over the shrouded sun."

How the harmonies strain the fetters of prose, and almost quiver into song! Perhaps it is as a poet of Nature that Meredith touches his highest felicity. Even in this pagan age, none since Wordsworth has knelt at the shrine of the mighty mother with more intense ardour of devotion; none has painted more faithfully or with more insight the flying moods of field and sky. The breath of English meadows, the intoxication of "the bared bosom of June", fills poems and novels alike; they teem with the luxuriance of leaf and blossom and fruitage. The very pulse of earth throbs through *Love in the Valley* or *The Day of the Daughter of Hades*. Understanding is born of love. The ears of Meredith, as those of his own Melampus, are unclosed to the voice of birds, and to the sob of ocean. He is initiate in the mysteries; the incommunicable secret, the peace of Demeter, is his. Feeling is urgent for translation into thought, and in Meredith's philosophy, harmony with nature becomes the great panacea, the sovereign remedy for the ills of life. Diana finds oblivion of her hunters among the clouds and flowers of Copsley, and the springs of Rhoda's strength flow from the Kentish meads of Queen Anne's farm, "wherein the red sorrel topped the yellow buttercups, like rust upon the season's gold".

The subject, however, of this essay is neither the national poetry, nor the poetry of Nature; it is the single poem which gave the name to the memorable volume of 1862. In *Modern Love*, more definitely than elsewhere, the vital points of the Meredithian attitude to life may be traced. It sets forth, in clearer outlines and sharper relief, the root-ideas that underlie *Diana* and *The Egoist*, and the other great tragedies. These ideas may be very briefly summed up. Meredith's thought is dominated by a sense of the eternal irony of life, the irony which plays around the struggle of human heart and human will against the fetters of natural law. Encountered in its various aspects, this irony yields both comedy and tragedy, hardly indeed distinct, for the fount of laughter lies very near the well of tears. Meredith's consciousness of the potency of law is absolute and uncompromising. It is forced upon him alike by his acute psychology and by his candid acceptance of the results of science. These are at one in their teaching. It is easy to recognize the ape and the tiger as ancestors of man, when you have analysed the presence of ape and tiger in man as he exists. Law then is supreme, and with law, according to Meredith, the higher life of man is eternally at issue. And here his idealism comes in to point the irony. His eye is sure to see, and his hand steady to paint all that is noble in human character and pure in human passion; yet his noblest and his purest are entangled in the web of fate, hounded into wrong-doing, or at the least, into misery. Of fate, yet of a fate that is self-conditioned; for the law that enchains man is not an external necessity, but an internal one, due to the presence of lower elements inter-mingled with the higher in his own being; here, the actual imperfection, there, the capacity of aspiring to what is per-fect. Character is subdued by a destiny that is itself the child of character, and therefore ineluctable, Aeschylean.

> In tragic life, God wot,
> No villain need be! Passions spin the plot:
> We are betrayed by what is false within.

Yet Meredith does not rest in an impotent creed of pessi-mism. Release from the struggle with Nature can indeed be won, but only by acquiescence in her decrees; and this not a passive acquiescence, not the vegetative content of those who "have the secret of the bull and lamb", the Gammons of life, whose "clod" no "spark" has ever yet disturbed, but a transcendent acquiescence, a harmony based on submission and understanding. Above all, understanding. The initial need for man is "more brain, more brain", that he may rise to full consciousness, first of his own powers and ideals, and then of the limitations that hedge these in. So alone can he become at one with Nature, and so shall he find her responsive, lady of unexpected soothing and undreamed-of delights.

In *Modern Love* the remedy is not presented; there is but a vague, elusive hint of it. The essential tragedy of life—that is carefully set forth in the history of two souls, laid bare with a psychological scalpel, painfully, but in infinite pity. The principal *dramatis personæ* are a husband and wife. Marriage for them has been the crown of impassioned courtship. For a while they were happy. The ways of life stretched out green before them.

> Lovers beneath the singing sky of May,
> They wandered once; clear as the dew on flowers.

They were one another's best, and the earth sang around them. Intellect was well matched with beauty and all beholders applauded a model pair. Each took life seriously upon a high plane of sentiment; each was idealist to the core. And—they hardly knew how it grew up—but this very fact began to drive them slowly asunder. They could not live wholly in the present; each in secret tried to scrutinize a doubtful future. And when ideals clashed, they knew no compromise: they would have their star all in all, or not at all. But when two are gathered together, the ideals are sure to clash, sooner or later. With our two it came thus. He conceived of love as going hand in hand with loyal life. He would play his part on some high stage, would fling down his gauntlet in the battlefield.

> My crime is, that the puppet of a dream,
> I plotted to be worthy of the world.

But for her love would brook no rival, accept no divided homage. "Love's jealous woods about the sun are curled". To give the whole of her, to have the whole of him, that was her dream. Beautiful ideals both, but unfortunately not compatible. And so the first spring in him of ambition to make his place in life came to her as disillusion: she held herself forgotten, neglected. And he the while absorbed in his new interests and strangely blind, she betook herself, heart-sick, to "the drugs that crowd about a woman's hand",

seeking anodyne for regret in imagined pleasures and deliberate excitements. Then came in the inevitable third, to whom
in some moment of pique or passion she yielded. At this
point the action of the poem begins. The story is told in fifty
sonnets—or rather pseudo-sonnets, for there are sixteen
instead of the orthodox fourteen lines—each of which mirrors
some mood or crisis in the man's soul-drama. They are
difficult of interpretation, for this reason, that the wife's
history is only indirectly presented, through the medium of
the husband's misunderstandings; and therefore we have
to read between the lines, and to reconstruct it for ourselves
out of partial and often distorted reflections. I have changed
my own mind about it more than once, and do not feel sure
that I have got it quite correctly now. In one black night the
truth that they are no longer one is flashed upon the man
from the wife's secret tears.

> By this he knew she wept with waking eyes:
> That, at his hand's light quiver by her head,
> The strange low sobs that shook their common bed,
> Were called into her with a sharp surprise,
> And strangled mute, like little gaping snakes,
> Dreadfully venomous to him. She lay
> Stone-still, and the long darkness flowed away
> With muffled pulses. Then, as midnight makes
> Her giant heart of Memory and Tears
> Drink the pale drug of silence, and so beat
> Sleep's heavy measure, they from head to feet
> Were moveless, looking through their dead black years,
> By vain regret scrawled over the blank wall.
> Like sculptured effigies they might be seen
> Upon their marriage-tomb, the sword between;
> Each wishing for the sword that severs all.

From the morrow, the whole tenour of their life is changed.
No word passes between them; but he has leapt to the true
conclusion, that she has been unfaithful to him, and with it
to the false conclusion that she has transferred the heart that
was his to another. The discovery makes shipwreck of his
soul. She becomes to him the incarnation of baleful beauty,
a malign Lilith among women!

> A star with lurid beams, she seemed to crown
> The pit of infamy.

In the necessary intimacy of married life the sight of her loveliness is at times a maddening temptation, but his sense of the sacredness of love is so high that he dares not treat her as a wife when the inner bond is broken.

> Lord God, who mad'st the thing so fair,
> See that I am drawn to her even now!
> It cannot be such harm on her cool brow
> To put a kiss? Yet if I meet him there!
> But she is mine! Ah, no! I know too well
> I claim a star whose light is overcast:
> I claim a phantom-woman in the Past.
> The hour has struck, though I heard not the bell!

His agony sweeps through all moods from revenge to pity. At one moment he finds it hard to hold himself from killing her; at another, he has tears for his knowledge of the struggles she must have gone through. But mainly, he thinks he does well to be angry. She has emptied the world for him and seems not to understand her deed. A sudden day in spring when "the golden foot of May is on the flowers", as it had been—before, startles him with its inappropriateness: he wonders to find it wake no ember of regret in her. In the meantime his own self-respect is unimpaired; the past is poisoned for him; but he would not be himself if he sought to forget it.

> the mocking Past will stay:
> And if I drink oblivion of a day,
> So shorten I the stature of my soul.

All interests which might have filled the void prove barren of consolation. He requires Philosophy to cast out Passion, but Philosophy is a prize that can only profit the young, and can only be won by the old:

> Not till the fire is dying in the grate,
> Look we for any kinship with the stars.

He strives to school himself in the book of Nature, to accept

the transitoriness of human affections as part of the immut-
able law of things. The head approves the doctrine, but the
heart revolts.

> 'I play for Seasons; not Eternities!'
> Says Nature, laughing on her way. 'So must
> All those whose stake is nothing more than dust!'
> And lo, she wins, and of her harmonies
> She is full sure! Upon her dying rose,
> She drops a look of fondness, and goes by,
> Scarce any retrospection in her eye;
> For she the laws of growth most deeply knows,
> Whose hands bear, here, a seed-bag—there, an urn.
> Pledged she herself to aught, 'twould mark her end!
> This lesson of our only visible friend,
> Can we not teach our foolish hearts to learn?
> Yes! yes!—but, oh, our human rose is fair
> Surpassingly! Lose calmly Love's great bliss,
> When the renewed for ever of a kiss
> Whirls life within the shower of loosened hair!

Yet another remedy offers itself, but one that can only renew
agony in self-contempt. He has looked upon a certain lady
whose hair is golden and her lips red and her speech witty,
and his wife shows signs of jealousy. It may be that her light
love is returning to him. If so, he can be revenged and "hurt
her cruelly". But how can he set the timepiece of his heart
to beat in unison with that of a new woman. Such love would
be perilously near to lust.

> Sure, that's one way Love drifts into the mart
> Where goat-legged buyers throng.

So, for the while, the thought is put aside. In the meantime,
both for the man and the woman the suffering has grown
intense, all the more because no word passes between them
on the subject that fills the thought of each. The sympathy
which alone makes communion of intimate things possible
has vanished, and neither can speak out. Once only, he puts
into her hand a letter, which he regards as a proof of her
falseness. The change in their relations is unapparent to the
outer world, which believes them to be lovers as of old. They

play their parts in the comedy—"HIDING THE SKELETON, shall be its name" with such consummate art as to extort each other's profound admiration. One day a boyish friend, flushed with the fervour of the dawn of love, begs for their blessing. They answer him with light chaff, until suddenly the wife falls to the ground.

> When she wakes,
> She looks the star that thro' the cedar shakes:
> Her lost moist hand clings mortally to mine.

This scene is followed by another in a country-house at Christmas. "The great carouse Knocks hard upon the midnight's hollow door", and they lie apart, intensely conscious of each other, and full of bitter remembrance.

> I know not how, but shuddering as I slept,
> I dreamed a banished angel to me crept;
> My feet were nourished on her breasts all night.

And now a new act in the tragedy begins. The man's conception of his wife has veered round again. Curiously inverting the real truth, he has come to believe that her flesh has been pure throughout, that her sin has been only against love. Yet this is even bitterer to him than the other would have been; and, though she be now repentant, and suing mutely for forgiveness, he cannot bring himself to forgive. He deems his own love dead, dead in agony, and she who has "made Love bleed", she must "bear all the venom of his tooth". Thus he puts himself in the wrong, and from this moment his whole nature degenerates. Again the golden-haired woman crosses his path, and this time he does not resist her. He speaks and thinks of her as "My Lady", of his wife as "Madam". For a while his soul vibrates between the two. His new love is a passive and a purely selfish one. My Lady is both wise and witty: she attracts him by the head rather than the heart, and flatters what is Satanic in him by a tribute of admiration, as of the sunflower to the sun. He conceives something of a passion for her, and yet he is not content.

> Am I failing? For no longer can I cast
> A glory round about this head of gold.

Glory she wears, but springing from the mould
Not like the consecration of the Past!
Is my soul beggared? Something more than earth
I cry for still: I cannot be at peace
In having Love upon a mortal lease.
I cannot take the woman at her worth!
Where is the ancient wealth wherewith I clothed
Our human nakedness, and could endow
With spiritual splendour a white brow
That else had grinned at me the fact I loathed?
A kiss is but a kiss now! and no wave
Of a great flood that whirls me to the sea.
But, as you will! we'll sit contentedly,
And eat our pot of honey on the grave.

The note of the unconquerable idealist rings through the
first eight lines of this sonnet. But idealism must have its
anodyne. He elaborates a cynical philosophy. "Nature is
remorseless, Love an illusion; let us live as scientific animals",
he cries, in strange parody of the true Meredithian creed.
Yet, the casuistry over, he still finds a gulf in his soul that
My Lady is powerless to fill up.

One restless corner of my heart or head,
That holds a dying something never dead.

Madam is often in his thoughts, although he thinks she is
nothing to him. He sees her suffer, but will not spare her.
Only commonplaces pass between them, and, when they
must needs speak:—

Our chain on silence clanks,
Time leers between, above his twiddling thumbs.

Then there is a lull in the action. "Our tragedy, is it alive or
dead?" Very soon, it proves to be intensely living. My Lady's
dominion over her lover grows. When she is there, his
soul is "arrowy to the light" in her. He presses her hard,
and at last she gives herself to him.

She yields: my Lady in her noblest mood
Has yielded: she, my golden-crownëd rose!
The bride of every sense! more sweet than those
Who breathe the violet breath of maidenhood.

O visage of still music in the sky!
Soft moon! I feel thy song, my fairest friend!
True harmony within can apprehend
Dumb harmony without. And hark! 'tis nigh!
Belief has struck the note of sound: a gleam
Of living silver shows me where she shook
Her long white fingers down the shadowy brook,
That sings her song, half waking, half in dream.
What two come here to mar this heavenly tune?
A man is one: the woman bears my name,
And honour. Their hands touch! Am I still tame?
God, what a dancing spectre seems the moon!

The unexpected meeting strikes him with a sudden sense of
unrest. He attempts to analyse his own shifting emotions,
and discovers with dread that the love which he had believed
gone for ever out of his life has still its old power over him.

Terrible Love, I ween,
Has might, even dead, half sighing to upheave
The lightless seas of selfishness amain:
Seas that in a man's heart have no rain
To fall and still them.

He finds himself "helplessly afloat", ignorant whither to
turn for peace.

So ends the second act. The ten closing sonnets are the
most difficult in the poem, for the rapid and complex changes
of thought and feeling that they shadow forth. The outline
of the story, as it suggests itself to at least one reader, is as
follows. In a pang of jealousy, the husband leaves My Lady,
who disappears from the scene, and returns to his wife. No
sooner has he done this than he regrets it. And moreover,
he has once more revised his beliefs about her: he thinks that
she too is hankering after her lover, that they both "have
taken up a lifeless vow To rob a living passion". He foresees
nothing but further misery for them ahead. Then comes a
night when it is suddenly revealed to him that her love is
for him alone. Still believing his own heart to be elsewhere,
he allows himself to be overmastered by her beauty.

Thoughts black as death,
Like a stirred pool in sunshine break. Her wrists

I catch: she faltering, as she half resists,
'You love . . . ? love . . . ? love . . . ?' all in an indrawn breath.

On the morrow, such "unblest kisses" bring remorse. Again the two remain silent and estranged, while he imagines that what he feels for her is not love but pity, until one morning "about the sounding of the Matin-bell", he finds her gone, and follows her to a well-remembered wood.

                                    I moved
    Toward her, and made proffer of my arm.
    She took it simply, with no rude alarm;
    And that disturbing shadow passed reproved.
    I felt the pained speech coming, and declared
    My firm belief in her, ere she could speak.
    A ghastly morning came into her cheek,
    While with a widening soul on me she stared.

With generous impulse he recognizes that her presence there was but to give dismissal. He avows his confidence in her purity throughout, and fails, so I understand it, to realize the shame which that avowal calls up in her. They commune together; they "drink the pure daylight of honest speech"— with one reservation; and the day of reconciliation closes with a marvellous sonnet. He has found himself now, and the harmonies of life are restored again.

    We saw the swallows gathering in the sky,
    And in the osier-isle we heard their noise.
    We had not to look back on summer joys,
    Or forward to a summer of bright dye:
    But in the largeness of the evening earth
    Our spirits grew as we went side by side.
    The hour became her husband and my bride.
    Love that had robbed us so, thus blessed our dearth!
    The pilgrims of the year waxed very loud
    In multitudinous chatterings, as the flood
    Full brown came from the West, and like pale blood
    Expanded to the upper crimson cloud.
    Love that had robbed us of immortal things,
    This little moment mercifully gave,
    Where I have seen across the twilight wave,
    The swan sail with her young beneath her wings.

But after all this is a tragedy, and must end tragically. The sin and the misunderstanding have been too great to be lightly put aside. The afterglow of love fades away into closing gloom. He has made his confession and received his pardon, when she leaves him once more. Suspecting some Quixotic resolve to set him free to fly to My Lady, he follows her and finds her " by the ocean's moaning verge".

> And she believed his old love had returned,
> Which was her exultation, and her scourge.

He leads her home, and it becomes apparent that all is not clear between them yet. There is some dire secret which she cannot tell him.

> But there's a strength to help the desperate weak.
> That night he learned how silence best can speak
> The awful things when Pity pleads for Sin.
> About the middle of the night her call
> Was heard, and he came wondering to the bed.
> 'Now kiss me, dear! it may be, now!' she said.
> Lethe had passed those lips, and he knew all.

If I am right in my interpretation of the poem, this secret, this intolerable burden on the wife's conscience, is nothing else than her initial sin of bodily unfaithfulness. This sin, the fruit not of an estranged soul, but of some moment of heart-sickness, when love seemed to have foundered, and honour and self-respect to be hardly worth saving from the wreck, she has long since bitterly repented of. Her husband's words in the wood have shown her that he is completely ignorant of it, that, having realized that her heart has always been his, he has acquitted her of any wrong against him. She cannot leave him in this ignorance and return to her old place, when he on his side has confessed. The stain upon her soul requires its confession and its expiation, and these it at last finds together in the eloquent silence of death. The ultimate reconciliation for these broken lives can only be a momentary thing. A concluding sonnet points the lesson of the whole:

> Thus piteously Love closed what he begat:
> The union of this ever-diverse pair!

These two were rapid falcons in a snare,
Condemned to do the flitting of the bat.
Lovers beneath the singing sky of May,
They wandered once; clear as the dew on flowers:
But they fed not on the advancing hours:
Their hearts held cravings for the buried day.
Then each applied to each that fatal knife,
Deep questioning, which probes to endless dole.
Ah, what a dusty answer gets the soul
When hot for certainties in this our life!—
In tragic hints here see what evermore
Moves dark as yonder midnight ocean's force,
Thundering like ramping hosts of warrior horse,
To throw that faint thin line upon the shore!

The inevitable tragedy of the idealists of this world; aspiring creatures, that cannot recognize or accept the necessary limitations of terrene existence. The law of Nature, which is Acquiescence, they know not, and once impeded in their flight, they push desperately and blindly on into the tangles of sorrow and sin. Until at last the wounded eagle falls into the mire, nor can ever again recover that primal potency of glorious wing. It is majestic poetry and a hard philosophy.

1897

MEREDITH'S NATURE POETRY

THOUGH a close lover of Nature, Mr. Meredith is no Thoreau, dwelling apart from humanity by the margin of his lake or in the shy recesses of the woods. How could he be, who in a dozen novels has kept such narrow watch and ward over the hearts of men? And in his poetry, too, the anachoretic ideal has no place. Human life and the riddle of it are to him of supreme interest. He is of those

> who hither, thither fare
> Close interthreading Nature with our kind;

and if he shuns cities, and seeks diurnal contact with the mind of the Great Mother, this is not solely for his personal refreshment, but that he may bring to the human hive the lessons of the sane and austere philosophy which a "reading of earth" affords. Some hint of this garnered wisdom the present essay may perhaps suggest.

Life presents itself to Mr. Meredith's acute analysis as a very tragic thing; an eternal conflict of the will and aspirations of man with the iron necessity of natural laws. The failure of the idealist—that is one of his favourite themes: and the spectacle becomes the more ironic, because the laws which determine failure are usually rooted in the sufferer's own personality, come of his weaknesses and imperfections.

One might illustrate this from any of the novels; better still, perhaps, from the poem called "Modern Love". Here is a tragedy in sonnets. The subject is the drifting apart of two who began life in a golden haze. Each had noble dreams and—oh! the irony of it—the dreams diverged. For her, love must be self-sufficient, leaving no room for external interests. For him, it could not exclude a strenuous share in the high activities which make their claim on man.

> In Love's deep woods,
> I dreamt of loyal Life:—the offence is there!
> Love's jealous woods about the sun are curled;
> At least, the sun far brighter there did beam.—

> My crime is, that the puppet of a dream,
> I plotted to be worthy of the world.
> Oh, had I with my darling helped to mince
> The facts of life, you still had seen me go
> With hindward feather and with forward toe,
> Her much-adored delightful Fairy Prince!

And so, throughout the magnificent evolution of the poem, you watch the rift widening. Misunderstanding grows upon misunderstanding: the "hooked and winged" thing, the "scaly dragon-fowl" that lies in wait obscurely deep in every soul asserts itself, and the tangle grows beyond putting right. And all through the failure to see life clearly, to grasp and accept its limitations. So, at least, one reader reads the story, and the final sonnet, or envoy, would seem to justify the interpretation:

> Thus piteously Love closed what he begat:
> The union of this ever-diverse pair!
> These two were rapid falcons in a snare,
> Condemned to do the flitting of the bat.
> Lovers beneath the singing sky of May,
> They wandered once; clear as the dew on flowers:
> But they fed not on the advancing hours:
> Their hearts held cravings for the buried day.
> Then each applied to each that fatal knife,
> Deep questioning, which probes to endless dole.
> Ah, what a dusty answer gets the soul
> When hot for certainties in this our life!—
> In tragic hints here see what evermore
> Moves dark as yonder midnight ocean's force,
> Thundering like ramping hosts of warrior horse,
> To throw that faint thin line upon the shore!

If this, then, is life, is there any remedy which may purge away the tragedy, or at least teach man to endure? Assuredly, says Mr. Meredith, if man will but learn of Nature. It is Melampus, the wise physician, to whom the secrets of birds and flowers have been revealed, who is

> luminous-eyed for earth and the fates
> We arm to bruise or caress us.

And the wisdom of Nature is in acceptance. It must be

catholic, not discriminating. Mr. Meredith loves the bracing
of shrewd Nature no less than the cheer of boon Nature.
And hence a law for the spiritual as well as the physical
perception.

> Accept, she says; it is not hard
> In woods; but she in towns
> Repeats, accept.

It is by meeting adversity that man learns, and by triumphing
over his senses.

> Master the blood, nor read by chills,
> Earth admonishes.

You attain by effort. "Follow the way of the husbandman";
press on, not seeking for spiritual anodynes, or questioning
too curiously of the "Whither" and the "Whence", but
setting hand strenuously to what lies there to be done.

> Contention is the vital force,
> Whence pluck they brain, her prize of gifts,
> Sky of the senses! on which height,
> Not disconnected, yet released,
> They see how spirit comes to light,
> Through conquest of the inner beast.

And when the spiritual apprehension has replaced the prick-
ing of the sense in man, then he has attained the permitted
success. He is armed for his fate. "Never is earth misread by
brain."

The root-ideas, here roughly indicated, seem to us to
underlie all Mr. Meredith's nature poetry on its philosophical side. They receive, perhaps, their most formal
and deliberate expression in two poems worthy of the most
patient study—*The Woods of Westermain* and *A Faith
on Trial*. The briefest of analysis may be attempted. The
woods of Westermain are the mystic woods of life. To the
confident wayfarer they give a wonderful invitation:

> Enter these enchanted woods,
> You who dare.
> Nothing harms beneath the leaves
> More than waves a swimmer cleaves.

> Toss your heart up with the lark,
> Foot at peace with mouse and worm,
>   Fair you fare.
> Only at a dread of dark
> Quaver, and they quit their form:
> Thousand eyeballs under hoods
>   Have you by the hair.
> Enter these enchanted woods,
>   You who dare.

The metaphor is kept, and the visions of delight vouchsafed to those properly equipped to see them dwelt upon. To them is unfolded "the heaven of things". They are in the world, and not of it.

> Sharing still its bliss and woe;
> Harnessed to its hungers, no.

They may read deep in the book of Nature, and get some glimpse of her impenetrable designs. But the condition is that the right faculty be brought to bear—soul, not sense.

> Look you with the soul you see 't.

Not that the senses are denied their share: the old interpretations of the morning of time are not barred by "the sterner worship".

> Banished is the white Foam-born
> Not from here, nor under ban
> Phoebus lyrist, Phoebe's horn,
> Pipings of the reedy Pan.

On the contrary, the spiritual apprehension gives a new reality, a new permanence, to that of sense. The young blood-heat, brought to measure, feeds a larger self. Love, above all, finds thus for the first time its proper meaning: the old battle of the sexes is dissolved in the taming of man and the exaltation of women.

> Goddess, is no myth inane,
> You will say of those who walk
> In the woods of Westermain.

But remember the caution: a false note in the temper of him

who ventures is the sign of discords. He must move rightly attuned.

> You must love the light so well
> That no darkness will seem fell.
> Love it so you could accost
> Fellowly a livid ghost.

This is the clue of it, which makes development to the higher plane possible. And always waiting is the snare of the lower self, the old Dragon, often riven, never slain. He too, however, shall some day be tamed, shall forget the "mine and thine", and shall serve reason. What, then, is the goal of development, "the fount and lure o' the chase"? It is the right apprehension of the meaning of Nature, the reading of her riddle. Men seek to know her in many ways, and in all the self of sense has its word. She gives no answer; is all flux, an inscrutable and remorseless succession of sowing and reaping, life and death. But this is the fault of the questioner.

> See you so? your senses drift;
> 'Tis a shuttle weaving swift.
> Look with spirit past the sense,
> Spirit shines in permanence.

Only through reason can man see Nature as she is: and then she becomes the key to every doorway. The tangle of the serpent vanishes with the misprision of earth; and the sane pleasures of blood, brain and spirit endure. Man pays his debt, and leaves to earth the future task. Nor is she slow to reward.

> Eglantine that climbs the yew,
> She her darkest wreathes for those
> Knowing her the Ever-new,
> And themselves the kin o' the rose.

Thus is the inmost of life and of its ardours made manifest, through the steady pursuit of light. Thus the man becomes rooted in earth; no glooms in Westermain can ever appal: and from the heights the tidal world is seen as it is, reconciled from its ebb and flow. Lines near the end of the poem give once more the warning.

> Are you of the stiff, the dry,
> Cursing the not understood;

Then,

> You are lost in Westermain:
> Earthward swoops a vulture sun,
> Nighted upon carrion:
> Straightway venom winecups shout
> Toasts to One whose eyes are out.

The sustained metaphor and wealth of subordinate imagery in *The Woods of Westermain* make it, in my opinion, one of the most difficult, as it is one of the fullest, of poems. *A Faith on Trial* is more direct, simpler in expression, and charged with the pathos of a personal note. It falls into two parts. The first, which is one of the most beautiful things, and certainly the most intimate thing, which Mr. Meredith has written, lies a little outside the scheme of this discussion. It is the narrative of an experience. The sentence of death hangs over the poet's wife. It is May-day, and he carries his numbed heart into the accustomed wild-wood ways:

> And around
> The sky was in garlands of cloud,
> Winning scents from unnumbered new births,
> Pointed buds, where the woods were browned
> By a mouldered beechen shroud;
> Or over our meads of the vale,
> Such an answer to sun as he
> Brave in his gold; to a sound,
> None sweeter, of woods flapping sail,
> With the first full flood of our year,
> For their voyage on lustreful sea:
> Unto what curtained haven in chief,
> Will be writ in the book of the sere.

But for the poet, the message of earth is lost on this morning. He sees, but it is only with the outward eye, by disciplined habit. He broods over

> sensations that make
> Of a ruffled philosophy rags.

Earth has become to him no longer "a Mother of grace", but "a Mother of aches and jests". Then he describes the change in his mood wrought by the sudden vision of a white wild cherry in bloom against a background of yews on the slope of the down; how it brings him back to faith, and once more, on the strength of his reading of earth, he accepts.

The second part of the poem is more abstract: it sets forth the wisdom "rough-written, and black" that came with the peace in the soul. The teaching should be by now familiar. Only then is man "orb to the greater whole" when the brain takes the place of the rebel heart, "our lord of sensations at war". Nature has no ready pity, gives no tear for tear. To "flesh in revolt" she has no promise and no word.

> We are asking her wheels to pause.

To those who seek easy consolation in the creeds and legends she is equally implacable:

> She yields not for prayers at her knees;
> The woolly beast bleating will shear.

The only way to win "her medical herb" is through seeing and hearing, through the real. Accept both death and life: let reason grapple with the "old worm, Self": front the "sacred Reality": and you have passed the ordeal of faith. Then follows a glorification of reason. The legends are nothing, and the questionings are nothing; Nature is all. And by reason Nature must be won.

> men by the lash made lean,
> Who in harness the mind subserve,
> Their title to read her have earned;
> Having mastered sensation—insane
> At a stroke of the terrified nerve;
> And out of the sensual hive,
> Grown to the flower of brain;
> To know her a thing alive,
> Whose aspects mutably swerve,
> Whose laws immutably reign.

The poem closes with a message of Earth to her children, a promise to the idealists who press on untiring to their "Dream of the blossom of good".

So meagre a summary will have served its purpose if it

finds new readers for some of the most tonic and helpful of modern poetry. Mr. Meredith's is a great personality. He is an optimist, but his optimism is no facile optimism: it derives from temperament, and is fortified by contemplation. And surely to renew the springs of optimism, to refresh a wilting faith, is one of the most legitimate functions of a singer-seer.

1898.

ALICE MEYNELL'S "RHYTHM OF LIFE"

ONE HAS, of course, an immense admiration for Mr. Henley, for the poetry and the brilliant individuality of the man. And yet it is hard to satisfy oneself that the many who have found in him an artistic stimulus must not go farther before they find also their artistic conscience. These clever young writers who pullulate around him—is it not his perversities that they catch, rather than his inspiration? And does he take the trouble to demur, when they sacrifice on the altar of a style alike the decencies of journalism and the dignities of literature? In any case we must credit Mr. Henley, as his undeniable achievement, with the capture and revelation of Mrs. Meynell. For after the immortal letter to Mr. Hyde of Honolulu, was there anything more signal in his memorable editorship of the *National Observer* than certain gracious essays, packed with thought and vibrile with wit, which stood there amongst cheap satire and schoolboy impertinences, like the cool spaces of a bookshop sequestered from the bustle of frivolous Piccadilly? And when those essays reappeared in book form as *The Rhythm of Life*, who was there who failed to recognise the presence of a new and potent pen, of a fresh critical force to be reckoned with, of an imperative need to reconsider and readjust certain old critical tendencies from another and a striking point of view? Incidentally one learnt that this was not Mrs. Meynell's first venture in the pleasant ways of literature. Already, as Miss Alice Thompson, she had published in 1875 a volume of poems, which did not indeed hit the popular taste, but which were very highly esteemed by no mean critics—Mr. Ruskin, in particular, speaking of some of her work as "the finest things I have yet seen or felt in modern verse". And then Miss Thompson exercised the ultimate privilege of the maiden and the artist, and for fifteen years was silent; slowly pruning and maturing, we may suppose, the potentialities of a naturally quick spirit by submission to the twofold scholarship of life and letters, that so, when in the fullness of time she reluctantly spoke again, her words might be the choice fruit of the trained eye, and the disciplined brain, and the purified heart.

In attempting to analyse the impression which Mrs. Meynell's writing makes upon at least one reader, I shall not dwell at length upon her sex, and upon the fact that she is perhaps the first woman to make her way to the higher levels of criticism. Doubtless the last quarter of the present century will be known as the age of the awakening of women, of their successful claim to share in the wider and fuller life of the race, from which they have hitherto been, in the main, excluded. And with the conquest of life comes naturally the conquest of literature. One even hopes that women will soon cease to use the apology of a masculine pseudonym on their title-pages. But though Mrs. Meynell is clearly touched by the fine issues which the problem of the future of her sex at this moment presents—we are grateful to her for her woman's protest against the gross defacement of woman by the pen of Dickens and the pencil of Leech—yet I think that she has always held herself characteristically aloof from the more revolutionary phases of the movement. That brave desire to arraign the whole of society as man has made it, to

> Shatter it to bits, and then
> Remould it nearer to the heart's desire,

could not be expected to evoke much but pity and amusement in the mind of one whose consciousness of the past is so strong, and who knows that, for women as for Americans, there is no beginning, but only a continuity. This, indeed, is the first point in Mrs. Meynell's critical temperament to which I would call attention. She has that sense of inheritance, of oneness with the past, which only liberal scholarship can give. She has chosen great ancestors to defer to. Must she quote? It is by preference the most distinguished utterances of the most distinguished men. Nor does she ever forget what such a descent entails upon her, its responsibilities "in the chastity of letters and in the honour of life", its compulsion to keep her thought unstained by anything that is common or "mentally inexpensive". How much "a man of letters" means to her!—"judicious, judicial, disinterested, patient, happy, temperate, delighted". What a rare equipment to have even formed such an ideal! And how doubly rare in an age which has substituted reviews for criticism and University Extension lectures for education! We habitually write up to the top of our information; but Mrs. Meynell selects from her treasure-house; she has her reserves; she does not wish to tell us "all the grave things".

This insistence on the literary point of honour and a certain delicate psychology define Mrs. Meynell's critical attitude. Of what is hackneyed she will have nothing. "Habitualness", she says, "compels our refusals". Patent things, even patent truths, fail to arrest her; she prefers a more intimate, even if it be a lesser, truth; a truth that she can feel, that has some freshness about it, not a truth that she must merely accept and share. She will not willingly walk in the ways of common tread. Therefore she pushes analysis as far as it can be pushed, in the discrimination of subtle shades of sentiment, the exploration of secret distinctions, which the blunter sense would disregard. And analysis frequently issues in paradox; a paradox, however, which is not often merely verbal, belonging, as it does, to the order of her thought and the structure of her material. For it is invariably truth itself that she seeks, and not the affectations of truth. No one, indeed, will prick you with more mordant wit the bubble of an affectation; the affectation, for instance, that finds pathos in what is really humorous, or the affectation of an impressionism that has no impressions worth recording. In this close power of penetration lies her delicate critical instrument; for in criticism, as in portraiture, it is the little touches that count, the barely noticeable curves and crow's-feet, that hold the secrets of mental history, and build up the ultimate ineffaceable personality. Nor need Velazquez himself have been ashamed to own that "Portrait of a Gentleman" in the essay which is called "A Remembrance". Subtle herself, Mrs. Meynell demands some response of subtlety from her readers; she is difficult, because she is not facile. She is indeed unpardonable, because she requires, compels thought; compels even an effort of thought, grinds the edge of thought. And to-day we do not wish that thought should give us pause. We ask for books to satisfy easy mental processes, and not to awake complicated ones; because we do our reading hurriedly, in the railway train or at the British Museum, and have no time for the composure of an arm-chair or the contemplation of a library.

The subtlety of Mrs. Meynell's thinking determines also her vocabulary. She will not use synonyms as if they were equivalents, for she knows that usage is the deposit of history, and that cognate words have cognate and not identical meanings. It were, therefore, a conceit in her own vein to say that her epithets and turns of phrase are not obvious, and are inevitable. Her words are not inanimate counters, but have their characters and their colours. The *epitheton constans* is no temptation to her, nor will she reproduce the second-hand quaintnesses of Wardour Street. Her tendency, indeed, is all to the Latin derivatives, so cool and quiet, for "to possess that half of the language within which Latin heredities lurk and Romanesque allusions are at play is to possess the state and security of a dead tongue, without the death". She seeks in style qualities that control rather than stimulate, is careless to cry aloud in the market-place, will not be clamant, and would rather have you not suspect the measure of her resources, for the discretion of the art that conceals them. So that it will surprise you on analysis to find that she, who is never rhetorical, possesses and has used every artifice of rhetoric.

It is the first instalment, then, of one's claim for Mrs. Meynell, that she has the choicer equipment of a critic, the comprehensive experience of life and letters, the acute vision, the easy control of an exquisite medium. But from the absolute critics, the two or three who interpret to an age, more than this is required. Of such we ask in addition a unity, an organic unity, of purpose and of aim. Some fecund principle of thought, far-reaching in its scope, and bearing upon what is vital rather than what is accidental, this alone can give birth to a criticism that shall be creative, dynamic. For in the positive, not the negative, pole of criticism, in its power to modify the old mental attitude and to suggest the new, must always lie its highest achievement. Nor can the operation of this principle be limited to any one department of human activity; on all alike, on art, on letters, on conduct, it will have its shaping word. Such a principle underlies Mrs. Meynell's work. It is rooted in a certain austere philosophy. "The half is better than the whole", cried the Greek; and Mrs. Meynell, too, solves many problems by her willingness to accept and even appropriate the limitations of life. Of one whose "personality made laws for me" she says, "he had always prayed temperate prayers and harboured probable wishes". Her most frequent counsel is to do without. "I could wish", she tells us, "abstention to exist, and even to be evident, in my words". Criticism is made up of innumerable rejections; and, if even rejections trouble that composure which is the heart's attainable felicity, what of the things rejected? By exclusion alone can we preserve unrifled our treasury of quietness, exclusion on the one hand of the raw, the slovenly, the blatant; on the other, of the opulent, the ostentatious, the tormented. In all things it is to "the little less" that she would "recall a rhetorical world". In art she would cure the disease of ornament by the wholesome tonic of plain spaces; in nature she prefers to "the clamorous proclamation of summer in the English woods" those finer lines of an unrecognized Italy, "cypresses shaped like flames, tall pines with the abrupt flatness of their tops, thin canes in the brakes, sharp aloes by the roadside, and olives with the delicate acuteness of the leaf". To be simple—it is the simplest of all secrets; and who shall say that it is not worth preaching in a flamboyant age? And in virtue of this gospel of simplicities and silences we count Mrs. Meynell high among critics, and place her pregnant pages on the shelf beside the *Essays in Criticism* and the *Studies in the Renaissance*.

1896.

THE STUDY OF ENGLISH LITERATURE

IT IS a wise thing, before we plunge into any new study, to try and give ourselves some account of what it is that we mean by it, and what it is that we expect from it. And therefore an historical sketch of English literature opens rightly with a consideration of the nature and the value of literature in general. What can books do for us? and in what spirit ought we to read them?—those are the preliminary questions which we must ask. And the answers which we shall find to them may perhaps help to assure us that we are not following a vain quest, on a track that leads no whither, and may furnish some ideas that, if kept steadily in mind, will serve as guides and sign-posts throughout the journey.

In these days of scientific and technical education, it is perhaps necessary to make an apology for proposing literature as a desirable subject for study at all. There is a very common feeling abroad that books, and especially poetry-books, are not practical. You hear it said, "Science deals with *things*: literature deals only with *words*; surely it is better to study things rather than words, which are but the images and pale copies of things". Now if this were a true account of literature, if it really dealt only with words and in no sense with things, the study of it would certainly be a very empty and unprofitable exercise. It would then be indeed better to straightway shut up our Shakespeares and our Miltons, and to devote all our laborious nights and days to the museum or the workshop. And unfortunately literature is too often taught so as to give a real handle to this charge that is brought against it. It *is* made, and unwisely made, a mere matter of "words, words, words". We read the very greatest books in our schools, but we read them in the wrong spirit, not for the wisdom and the beauty that they contain, but only as so much raw material for lessons in philology and grammar. So that you may have a student of Vergil who is quite familiar with all the Greek constructions in the *Æneid*, and entirely

H

ignorant as to why the writer persistently calls Æneas "pious", or how that epithet is to be reconciled with the hero's conduct towards Dido; and a student of *Hamlet*, who would be quite prepared to write a page on the possible meanings of a "dram of eale", but would be sorely gravelled if you thought of asking him why Hamlet was so exceedingly disrespectful to the venerable Polonius. It cannot be too often repeated that to approach literature in this spirit is to approach it in the wrong spirit. It is like studying the picture of some great master simply as an illustration of anatomy, without paying any regard to the beauty of colour and design, or to the beauty of expression. A knowledge of bodily structure is essential to the artist, and useful even to the student of pictures, but it is not the only thing or the important thing to attend to. And similarly in literature, a knowledge of the history and structure of language is essential to the writer, and useful even to the student of books, but to treat it as the main object of study is only to mistake the proportion and the relative value of things.

But when this preference of the letter to the soul is put aside, and literature is studied with a right perception of its meaning and of the true significance of the various elements contained in it, then it declares itself as concerned by no means with words alone, but with things, in as real a sense as any science under the sun. For there are things in the world of a higher order than plants and stones and beetles, or anything that the microscope and the test-tube reveal to us; things spiritual, as well as things material and palpable; and with such things it is that literature has to do. Knowledge, like life itself, has its twofold aspect. There are the facts of organic and inorganic nature, upon which all the sciences are built; and beyond and above these there are the facts of consciousness, of man and of man's quick sight and subtle brain and aspiring soul. These, no less than the others, are worthy of study in their turn; and of these in all their intricate working, since the world grew articulate, literature is the witness and the imperishable record. Books there are, as Charles Lamb said, that are no books, *biblia a-biblia*; not alone "Court Calendars, Directories, Pocket-books", and the like, but whatsoever at any time has been written merely as a task for gain, with nothing in it of heart and nothing of soul. These are not literature; they vanish from memory, and only cumber our libraries. But the real books, the books that count and always will count, what are they but the spiritual history of humanity? For whenever, throughout the ages, a man has seen clearly, or has had a great thought, or has been thrilled with a splendid emotion, then he has straightway gone and put it in a book, that we who come after may see and think and feel with him. "Literature is a criticism of life", said Matthew Arnold, "because it preserves the best that has been known and thought in the world". "The best things, said in the best way", let that stand for our definition. And of literature, thus interpreted, the borders are wide. There is room in it for all that is written honestly and well, from the vast epic to the blind crowder's ballad. Men of all characters and all tempers, the grave historian and the light-hearted lyrist, the dreamer of high dreams, and the patient observer of some minute corner of real life; each, by simply giving the best that was in him, has helped to pile up the vast treasure which is the most precious inheritance of humanity. Therefore to read great books is to have the companionship of the aristocracy among the dead. We may be poor and of no account; our lives may be passed in sordid and vulgar surroundings; yet, if we will, we are welcome to the very best of society; we may escape from the prison of the self to breathe the diviner air, and in the heaven of "those who know" may share the meditations of Plato and of Dante. And in this fellowship with the great minds of the past, this intimacy with things lovely and of good report, there lies the true education. Plato himself saw this, when he would have none but noble poets and noble artists in his ideal city, "that so our young citizens, dwelling as it were in a boon clime, may drink in both by eye and ear the spirit of noble works; the very breeze itself blowing, you might say, from regions of health, and insensibly from their earliest years moulding them into harmony and conformity with beauty and with reason".[1]

[1] *Republic*, book iii. chap. 12.

But this educative power of literature, which Plato here speaks of, is something of which at the time we are hardly aware. Its influence upon us is an unconscious one, akin to that of the atmosphere, or of the common everyday sights of childhood. And there can be no doubt that an early familiarity, however uncritical and unsystematic, with great books is one of the forces which make most strongly for education. Insensibly, by ways silent and undreamt of, it informs the character and moulds the imagination. Wordsworth, in one of his most inspired passages, speaks of the quite similar workings of an early familiarity with the beauty and the mystery of external nature. "She shall be mine", he makes Nature say of Lucy:

> She shall be mine, and I will make
> A Lady of my own.
>
> Myself will to my darling be
> Both law and impulse: and with me
> The Girl, in rock and plain,
> In earth and heaven, in glade and bower,
> Shall feel an overseeing power
> To kindle or restrain.
>
> She shall be sportive as the fawn,
> That wild with glee across the lawn
> Or up the mountain springs;
> And hers shall be the breathing balm,
> And hers the silence and the calm
> Of mute insensate things.
>
> The floating clouds their state shall lend
> To her; for her the willow bend;
> Nor shall she fail to see
> Even in the motions of the Storm
> Grace that shall mould the Maiden's form
> By silent sympathy.
>
> The stars of midnight shall be dear
> To her; and she shall lean her ear
> In many a secret place
> Where rivulets dance their wayward round,
> And beauty born of murmuring sound
> Shall pass into her face.

Thus Wordsworth of Nature; and through books, especially such books as have the grandeur and simplicity of Wordsworth and of Nature, there is the same ready avenue to the stores of spiritual strength and spiritual consolation that lie at the heart of things. But with books as with Nature, there comes a moment when this uncritical, unsystematic acceptance, so valuable in childhood, no longer suffices us. We desire to drink a deeper draught of the Pierian spring, to surrender ourselves more completely and with fuller insight to that power which as yet we but dimly and vaguely feel. And the finer understanding of literature, to which we now aspire, does not, like the first childish intimacy, come without taking thought for it. To win that secret, as to win anything else that is worth possessing, calls for its renunciations and its arduous toils. The kingdom of heaven is not taken by storm. Would we learn the great language and catch the clear accents of the masters of speech and song, we must prepare ourselves for a task that requires no small time, and is attended by no small difficulties. There is that obvious difficulty, which presents itself in some measure in approaching the earlier literature of one's own country, and which becomes really serious when one approaches any part of the literatures of other peoples and other countries, the difficulty of accustoming oneself to an alien tongue and an alien idiom. This in itself is so considerable that, as has been pointed out, the surmounting of it is unfortunately too often taken as an end instead of as a means to the study of literature. And when, by the aid of grammar and dictionary and translation, this initial difficulty has been at least overcome, there still remains the further and perhaps even greater difficulty of learning to see what we read in its proper historical perspective. For no writer, however great, stands absolutely alone; each is the child of his own age, and the brother of his own people; nor is a complete understanding of any man's work possible, without some knowledge of the conditions under which it had its being, of the influences which helped to shape its form and inspire its purpose. This is an universal law. Wordsworth, indeed, says of Milton, "Thy soul was like a Star, and dwelt apart"; and in a sense this is true, not of

Milton alone, but of many another poet, the grandeur and purity of whose soul has outshone the petty and warped aims of lesser men, as the steadfast planet outshines the street-lamps. But it is not true if it is taken to mean that Milton or any of Milton's kin lived a life which was out of all relation to the common life of his own countrymen in his own day. The greatest are none the less, in their degree, subject to the ordinary limitations of humanity: their keenest vision cannot pierce far beyond the possibilities of existing know-ledge, nor their highest aspirations soar a pitch out of all reach of existing ideals: the spiritual interests of those around them, purified and widened, it may be, in scope, but still essentially the same, are theirs also, and in their noblest utter-ances they do but give fuller and more conscious expression to the very ideas which, in forms crude and ill-defined, sway the contemporary masses. And, therefore, as in a mirror, they "show the very age and body of the time his form and pressure". The annals of our country are written in its poets and novelists, no less than in its historians. As you pass from Chaucer to Spenser, and again from Spenser to Milton, the complete history of the Renaissance is unrolled before you; while in the pages of Shakespeare, and in a less measure in those of Pope or of Tennyson, you may find the abstract and brief chronicle of a whole epoch of national civilization. It is also of course true, and should not be forgotten, that the greater a writer is, the more he takes his stand upon certain broad humanities, which are not of an age, but for all time; and this may be thought to require some modification of what has just been said. The great elementary facts of exist-ence, birth and labour and death; the primal relations of man to God, of lover to maiden, of mother to child; these themes, and others like them, have been at the root of every literature throughout the centuries. Homer knew them, and our latter-day singers are not weary of them yet. But, common as they are, every people and every age has interpreted them for itself afresh, has shed upon them the light of its own peculiar senti-ment, and clothed them in the disguise of its own character-istic imagery. And so for each they have come to bear new and special forms, and to find expression in modes, which to

those outside must needs be, at first sight, strange and un-
familiar. At heart the *Oresteia* of Aeschylus and the *Macbeth*
of Shakespeare deal with the same problem, the eternal problem of sin and of sin's retribution. And yet how differently
it presents itself; what a world of thought and feeling lies
between the Greek of the fifth century before Christ, and the
Englishman of the seventeenth century after; how difficult,
how impossible, without an adequate knowledge of the
mental history of that two-thousand-years interval, to put
them on the same plane, and to realize how far they are
actually akin. It follows that one important object of the deliberate study of literature, as distinct from the casual and
uninstructed enjoyment of it, must be to remove these
obstacles which the inevitable lapse of time has set in our
way. Until this is done we shall always feel to some extent
strangers, when we wander outside the immediate domain
of contemporary prose and verse. And in the absence of an
historic background we shall hardly see even contemporary
prose and verse as they really are. But with these, no doubt,
the difficulty will be less. A modern writer must have links
with the past; but, still more, he must be of the present: on
the one side he may escape us, on the other he is necessarily
ours. By a reader of the present day, Browning is more
quickly appreciated than Spenser, although his thought is in
itself far more obscure and intricate. But then he speaks
directly to us, from our own point of view; we are in touch
with him from the beginning, whereas we have to *put* ourselves in touch with Spenser, exercising a quasi-dramatic
faculty, a painfully-acquired historic sense, which may
enable us to see as he saw, and to reconstruct for ourselves the
mental and social conditions under which he wrote. And the
acquirement of this historic sense or sympathy, difficult as it
is to attain to, is the indispensable method, if we are ever to
listen to Spenser, or any of the great voices of the past, at all.
Without it, they have nothing to say to us; with it, the barriers
fall down, and the mighty of every age are declared to be of
one heart and one tongue.

We may be certain, then, in the first place, of English
literature, that it should be treated in the closest connection

with English history. And, so treated, it is surely one of the most fascinating of all studies. For nowhere else, quite so clearly as in our books, may the many-sided, many-coloured genius of our nation be observed. The gradual development of this genius, the formation of the distinctively English temper out of isolated and warring elements, will be traced for us in the course of the present volume. We shall watch the coming together of the various racial stocks, each of them with its characteristic literary note, which constitute our ancestry. We shall see the imaginative fervour of the Celt, the sombre literalism of the Anglo-Saxon, the curious blend of gaiety and didacticism which marks the Norman-French, each in its turn absorbed into a whole, wherein all these divers qualities are still, as it were, held in solution, and uniting there to form a single spirit, flexible and richly endowed, with infinite capabilities for the widest range of feeling and expression. And in future volumes we shall find in the literature to which this spirit has given rise a mighty instrument, an organ responsive to every stirring event in the life of the people to which it belongs, voicing their hopes and fears, and reflecting every phase of action or speculation in which their unconquerable energy has found an outlet. And, though nationalism be thus of its heartblood, we shall not find it merely national, in any petty or exclusive sense, in its outlook. Always from time to time it has been ready to liberalize itself by contact with the ideas of other peoples. Above all it has gladly drunk in deep draughts of inspiration from the great literatures of the past, and thus, for all its innate vitality and romanticism, it has caught the classical accent, and has shown itself the heir across the centuries of "the splendour that was Greece, and the glory that was Rome". So that, in truth, the writers of our books have been the real leaders of our nation, holding it up a mirror of itself indeed, but at the same time lighting its beacon-fires, and pointing it onwards to the distant shining of new and ever new ideals.

Valuable, however, as the historical element in the study of literature is, it must always be borne in mind that it does not constitute the whole of that study. On the contrary, by emphasizing one side of the truth, it is apt to distort our view of the truth itself. For the historian is, of necessity, greatly occupied with large generalizations; he has to trace the growth and the working of influences and tendencies which affect a whole age or generation, and which are often most clearly discerned in the minor rather than in the major writers thereof. There is consequently always a danger lest these minor writers should receive a larger share of attention than their intrinsic merit would warrant. For after all, these influences and tendencies are chiefly significant to us because they lay down the conditions and supply the material from which the makers of literature take their start. They are common to the genius and the literary hack, the distinction between whom is essentially one, not of surroundings, but of individual temperament and individual character. Yet our study will have failed altogether in its purpose if we are led for one moment to neglect the existence or the importance of that distinction. Mediocrity is not the same thing as greatness, although we may have to spend much time over the consideration of mediocrity, in order to understand the conditions under which greatness had its rise. The forerunners and the imitators of Chaucer make up a large part of the literary history of the fourteenth and fifteenth centuries; but, nevertheless, the one vital event of that period is nothing other than the appearance of Chaucer himself; everything else is but secondary and subordinate to this. If then we desire to keep things in their true proportions, to focus correctly the figures of the motley procession that is to pass before us, we must take care to be well armed against these possible dangers of the historical spirit. And the surest of all safeguards is to preserve a high ideal of what supreme literary excellence consists in. If we once learn to know and love the highest when we see it, we shall not easily be led astray by what is merely specious or commonplace. Rarely, of course, shall we find writers who habitually and over a large mass of their work come up to the level of such an ideal; many who touch it once or twice only in their lives, still more who steadily and persistently fall beneath it. And even where the ideal is not wholly attained, there is much that is, in its degree, pleasant and profitable. But such a talisman, or touchstone of literary merit, is essential to guide us securely through the mazes of the historical survey. Nor is there any other royal road to acquire it than that of a close familiarity with the greatest masters, the familiarity that comes of reading them patiently and often, not for enjoyment merely, though we shall have much of this too in the process, but with the deliberate intention of discovering, so far as it may be discovered, the secret of their greatness; discovering it for ourselves in the first place, and in the second place steadying and rectifying our own judgment by what others have well and wisely said about them. In a word, if we are to understand literature and literary history aright, we must learn to approach them, not only as students, but as critics.

There have been and there are many misunderstandings as to the true meaning and nature of criticism. But it is safe to say that it does not mean the setting up of a system of hard-and-fast rules, and the condemning of everything which does not precisely conform to these, as for instance the French critics of the eighteenth century condemned every tragedy which did not precisely conform to the so-called tragic unities of place and time. And on the other hand, it is safe to say that it does not mean merely the expression of personal tastes and preferences. The man who "knows what he likes" is not on that account necessarily a critic. Certainly no criticism is worth much which is only borrowed, and is not based upon actual personal impressions. But then, to have a critical value, these must be the personal impressions of the right person, the person, that is, who is qualified by nature and by training to see things in their right light, as they really are. And this faculty of seeing things as they really are, in their right light and in their true proportions, is precisely what we require, in our study of literature, to correct the errors of the historical point of view. There are two functions, according to the original significance of the word *critic*,[1] which we must look to criticism and

---

[1] It is from κρίνειν to separate, and has therefore the two senses of (a) *divide*, as a judge (κριτής) divides the good from the bad, and (b) *distinguish, analyse, appraise, appreciate*.

to the development of our critical faculty to perform for us. The critic must be at once a judge and an appraiser. In so far as he is a judge, he must maintain that high ideal of supreme literary excellence which we have already seen to be so important and so desirable. He must keep green the eternal division set between what is literature, and what merely apes literature. He must single out from the great mass of what is imitative and undistinguished the little, the comparatively little, which really signifies. Not that certain classes of books are literature, and others not literature. It is not here that the difference lies. We have said that the borders of literature are wide; they do not admit the epic and exclude the familiar letter or the treatise on optics. We have no need to go beyond our definition of "the best things said in the best way". All that falls within this definition, of whatever kind it be, is literature; all that falls outside, except for the purpose of tracing links in the chain of historical development, is negligible. And the excellence of an epic, whether as regards what is said, or as regards the manner in which it is said, is not the excellence of the familiar letter or of the treatise on optics. But what the critic has to do, is to require of every book that it shall have the appropriate excellencies of its own species; of its matter, that it shall contain logical reasoning, or brave thoughts, or beautiful fancies, as the case may be; of its style, that it shall be, in the first place, a clear and transparent medium of ideas, and in the second, that it shall possess a comeliness of its own, and whether simple or adorned, shall reflect the virtues and graces of dignity, order, and melody. So much we expect from the critic in his capacity as judge, or guardian of our literary ideal. Nor does his second function of appraiser make any less severe demand upon his patience and his insight. No man's work is precisely the same as that of any other man; and whatever is worthy to be counted as literature at all has always its own characteristic notes, its own atmosphere, as it were, or perfume, dependent upon the presence of certain qualities of head and heart, which are not found in just that same combination anywhere else, and which are indeed the soul of the writer revealed and made manifest in play or poem. And it is

the task of the critic to gather up and interpret these dominant qualities, to reconstruct the human individuality from the
books, to distinguish and preserve, and, so far as it is com-
municable, to communicate to others, that unique and intimate fragrance. So that in the last resort he is a reader, not of
books only, but of souls, commissioned to explore the secrets
of personality, and to learn of singer and of saint, in the
words of Browning,

> how and why
> He differs from his fellows utterly.

In this spirit, then, of historical enquiry tempered with
criticism, let us take our plunge into literature, nothing
doubting that our books will be to us at all times the most
cunning of physicians and the best of friends.

1896.

THE TIMELESSNESS OF POETRY

IT IS difficult to speak of poetry, at a moment when civilization itself, of which poetry is the expression and the fine
flower, is in the balance. To the last war our young men went
singing:

> If I should die, think only this of me:
>   That there's some corner of a foreign field
> That is for ever England.

At the end, they were more disillusioned.

> Was it for this the clay grew tall?
> —O what made fatuous sunbeams toil
> To break earth's sleep at all?

There is not much singing now, even though maidens strewed
lilac branches on the roads, as the English troops once more
entered Belgium. Perhaps the present generation, with the
experience of their fathers behind them, are more conscious
of the grimness of the thing.

But I do not mean to say anything more to-day about war
and poetry. Let us, for an hour, have what the theologians
call a *refrigerium*, and think of poetry itself, as it has been
throughout the ages, and some day, perhaps, may be again.

The poets themselves have left us many true and illuminating sayings about their own function, as they conceived it.
"There is none in the universe", declared Tasso, "who
merits the name of a creator, save God and the Poet".
Poetry, our own Sidney tells us, adds something to nature.
"Nature never set forth the earth in so rich tapestry, as divers
Poets have done, neither with pleasant rivers, fruitful trees,
sweet-smelling flowers: nor whatsoever else may make the
too much loved earth more lovely". Those words make even
poetry itself more lovely. Shakespeare's poet is "of imagination all compact". Milton puts poetry before logic, as "more
simple, sensuous, and passionate". Wordsworth says that
"all good poetry is the spontaneous overflow of powerful

feelings", and again that "it takes its origin from emotion recollected in tranquillity". Shelley abounds in statements about poetry. It is "the expression of the imagination". It is "something divine". It is "the very image of life expressed in its eternal truth". It is "the perfect and consummate bloom of all things; it is as the odour and colour of the rose to the texture of the elements which compose it". It is "the record of the best and happiest moments of the best and happiest minds". It "turns all things to loveliness". I put these passages together, partly because the poets ought to know best what poetry is, but mainly because, although some of them are rhetorical rather than analytic, they illustrate the swing of emphasis between the elements of emotion and imagination, which are present in poetry, as in every other form of art. Coleridge, in the *Biographia Literaria*, approaching the question mainly from the philosophical standpoint, laid the stress upon imagination, but became involved in the metaphysics of imagination, and in an attempted distinction between imagination and fancy, which is little more than a matter of degree. In his later life he fell back upon what he called his "homely definitions" of prose and poetry, that is, for prose, "words in their best order", and for poetry, "the best words in their best order". That does not help us much, since by "the best words" Coleridge can only mean the best words, not for prose, but for poetry, which remains undefined. More recently A. E. Housman has declined to attempt an intellectual definition of poetry, and confined himself to describing the physical reactions which it evoked in him. He thought the production of poetry "less an active than a passive and involuntary process", and, if he must classify it, would call it a "secretion".

I, certainly, do not intend to attempt a watertight definition, where so many have failed. But at least we may accept it that in poetry there are two psychological elements involved. One is that of emotion, originally evoked by something given to the mind from without, either through the perception of an object, such as a landscape or a flower, or through reflection on a fact of life itself, such as birth or love or death; and intensified in the completed product by the operation of the

second element, the creative process of imagination, already
perhaps involved in perception or reflection themselves, even
if we do not accept the view of Coleridge that it is "a repetition
in the finite mind of the eternal act of creation in the infinite
I AM".

To take a very simple example. The poet starts from the
fact of a field full of yellow daffodils. He has a perception of
them, and their beauty causes emotion. Imagination gets to
work. The yellow is of gold. The daffodils are a host; they
are serried; they wave banners. New images come in and dis-
place this. They are stars in the Milky Way. They are
dancers. Both imagination and emotion are renewed in solitude. I am a dancer too. My heart dances with them. Poetry
then is a complex, of something given from without, and
something transforming it from within. It is *Homo additus
naturae*. Aristotle, like Tasso, was already conscious of the
creative element in it, and notes that *Poesis* is "making"
something, and for the full analysis of the interaction of
emotion and imagination in poetry, we must go to the psych-
ologists, notably to Samuel Alexander, in his lucid and
illuminating book on *Beauty and Other Forms of Value*,
although I think that he rather tends to over-emphasize the
element of imagination as compared with that of emotion.

Poetry is of course a form of art, and the impulse to poetry,
as to any other form of art, is part of the impulse to beauty,
one of the three great impulses which, according to the
philosophers, make up the humanity of man, and according
to some of them, bring man into contact with the divine.
The others are the impulse to knowledge and the impulse to
righteousness. Of the interaction between these civilization
is the outcome. But the three impulses are not equally pro-
gressive. Knowledge grows, but righteousness does not
seem to keep pace with it. Knowledge gave us the theory of
the internal-combustion engine, but our roads are a shambles,
and civilization itself is now at stake. This is by the way.
My immediate point is that the impulse to beauty also seems
to be an unprogressive one. We know more than the Greeks,
but we do not make more beautiful things, or write
more beautiful poetry. That is a large part of what I mean by

the timelessness of poetry. The forms of expression vary. Difficulties of dialect intervene. But essentially, throughout the ages, all poets use the same language, and are intelligible to one another. They acknowledge a common ancestry. Poetry comes down to us, like the blossoms. Mr. De La Mare has said what I want to say for me, far better than I can say it for myself. It takes a poet to speak properly of poetry.

> Very old are the woods;
>   And the buds that break
> Out of the briar's boughs,
>   When March winds wake,
> So old with their beauty are—
>   Oh, no man knows
> Through what wild centuries
>   Roves back the rose.

> Very old are we men;
>   Our dreams are tales
> Told in dim Eden
>   By Eve's nightingales.

My distinguished namesake, Dr. R. W. Chambers, has written, with far more learning than I can claim, an admirable essay on the continuity of English prose, from its beginnings to the Renaissance. I wish that I could similarly emphasize the continuity of English poetry, not only in itself, but in relation to the long story of classical and romance poetry that came before it. Many of my hearers are no doubt teachers of English literature, and are accustomed to classify it by periods, starting, I dare say, in view of the linguistic difficulties, not much earlier than Chaucer, or perhaps *Piers Plowman*, and conscientiously tracing the development through the Renaissance to a culmination in Shakespeare; then noting the new factors due to the emergence of the wit of Donne, and the French influence brought in by Dryden, lamenting perhaps the more prosaic age of reason dominated by Pope, and so on to the rise of what is called the romantic ideal, which has remained the chief force in poetry down to our own day. That is, no doubt, a useful exercise. Anything, indeed, will do as a scaffolding, so long as it is not forgotten that the educational purpose is to bring the young mind, in one way or another, directly into contact with poetry itself. But there are dangers in the historic method. The categories may easily become too rigid. There are waves, but the continuity of the tide is unbroken. This is very apparent in the wisely balanced study of Professor Elton's *The English Muse*. The period of Dryden, if it may be so called, does not begin until about the middle of the seventeenth century, and during the earlier part of it Vaughan, King, Marvell, Lovelace, Rochester, and others were still singing, to those who had ears to hear. Above all, Milton, as Professor Elton puts it, was working "alone in that mental solitude, which seems to be required for the production of great art". I gather that my distinguished predecessor in this office has little use for Milton, at any rate in his longer poems. Well, we all have our blind spots for poetry. Mine will, no doubt, become apparent before this discourse is finished. And, of course, even in the most prosaic days, Shakespeare never lost his pre-eminence. Dryden was unwearied in praising him, not indeed without criticism, some of which was justifiable. Both Pope and Johnson edited him —badly, it is true—but that was for want of philological equipment rather than for want of sympathy.

However, the prosaic period, in so far as it was one, may be said to have lasted to the middle of the eighteenth century. But long before there had begun what Professor Elton calls a "timid" return to nature, which was intensified later through the influence of Milton, after all more enduring than that of Pope, on Collins, Gray, Cowper, and lesser writers. It was reinforced by the interest in balladry due to Percy's edition of the *Reliques of English Poetry* in 1765, and by the end of the century the so-called romantic revival was in full swing. But here, too, I think, it is possible to over-emphasize the breach of continuity. The way had been smoothed for the romanticists by their immediate predecessors. Coleridge, of course, was strongly influenced by the ballad-writers, but Wordsworth derived more obviously from Milton and Shakespeare. The most marked revolutionary was Blake, who definitely tilted for the imagination as against the reason.

Let us, however, admit that there was a period when, for

their sins, men preferred versified prose to poetry. That is in any case no obstacle to the doctrine of the continuity, the timelessness, of poetry, in so far as poetry is to be found. Anywhere, throughout the ages, you may suddenly turn a page, and become conscious of its stab. And this continuity, or at least one aspect of it, may be further illustrated by the recurrence, century after century, of certain familiar themes, which have moved men's minds from the beginning, and, for all we know, will move them to the end.

Take, for example, the theme of Helen of Troy. The mythologists tell us that in origin she may have been divine, a *Koré* or earth maiden and mother, somewhere in the Aegean. The legend of her rape by Paris may have arisen in Thessaly. She was worshipped in Sparta, and her grave was shown to travellers, in a village hard by. But for us she is very human, the sheer creation of poetry itself. It was Homer who wrought the marvel. Leukolenos, he calls her, Helen of the white arms. She has little part in the action of the *Iliad*, although the whole story revolves round her. In the third book she sits with Priam in a tower above the Skaian gate. The people grumble at the trouble she has brought upon the city, but they speak winged words as they gaze at her. "Marvellous like she is to the immortal goddesses to look upon." With Priam she watches the Greek warriors as they move in the plain below, and tells him their names. But she does not see her own brothers, Kastor the tamer of horses, and Polydeukes the boxer, and she knows not that them the life-giving earth holds fast in Lakedaimon, in their dear native land. She is unhappy in Troy. Her fancy for Paris has gone, and her only friends are old Priam and the generous-hearted Hector. At the end of the story, when Hector is dead, she is there to speak the last word of lamentation over his body. We meet her again in the *Odyssey*, in that remarkable and curiously modern episode, where Telemachus, in search for his father Odysseus, comes to Sparta, and finds her there, restored to her husband Menelaus. There she sits,

The bright of women, Helen flowing-gowned,

just as any medieval or Elizabethan lady might sit, among her handmaidens, with her work-basket by her side. All that ancient trouble is now only a dim recollection, as she listens to the traveller's tale, and bids the couch be prepared for his repose.

Poetry has never forgotten Helen.   Dante, of course, places her in the second circle of his terrible *Inferno*, among the carnal sinners, Helen, who was the centre of so many ills.

> Elena vedi, per cui tanto reo
> Tempo si volse.

But it is her beauty, not her frailty, which has endured. She comes very early into our own literature, in that curious *Love Rune* of the thirteenth-century Franciscan, Thomas de Hales, who probably had the story, not direct from Homer, but from one of his medieval re-writers. It is one of those many *Ubi Sunt* poems, in which the ecclesiastic imagination was wont to emphasize the nothingness of earthly life by a bead-roll of its vanished glories.

Where is Tristram, where is Hector? And with them,

> Hwer is Paris and Heleyne
>   That weren so bryht and feyre on bleo,
> Heo beoth i-glyden vt of the reyne,
>   So the schef is of the cleo.

And ever since, the memory of Helen has run like a golden thread through our literature. For Chaucer she is an exemplar of beauty, only to be outdone by the subject of his own songs.

> Hyde ye youre beautes, Isoude and Eleyne,
> My lady cometh, that all this may disteyne.

The Earl of Surrey knows her, but serves "a worthier wight than she". Shakespeare is sometimes cynical about her, not only in *Troilus and Cressida*, where he is cynical about everything, but also in *As You Like It*, where, according to Orlando, Rosalind has "Helen's cheek, but not her heart", and in *Romeo and Juliet*, where Mercutio prophesies that Helen and Hero will be "hildings and harlots", when Romeo comes with his verses to Juliet. Here, however, the cynicism falls upon Helen's poets rather than upon Helen herself, and amends are made in *A Midsummer Night's Dream*, where the frantic lover

> Sees Helen's beauty in a brow of Egypt,

and in the fifty-third *Sonnet*, where Shakespeare's friend is told,

> On Helen's cheek all art of beauty set,
> And you in Grecian tires are painted new.

Marlowe, like Goethe after him, brings Helen into the Faust legend.

> Was this the face that launched a thousand ships,
> And burnt the topless towers of Ilium?
> Sweet Helen, make me immortal with a kiss.

She is in that rather unexpectedly lovely adieu to earth's bliss of the filibustering Nashe, written during a time of pestilence in London.

> Beauty is but a flower
> Which wrinkles will devour;
> Brightness falls from the air;
> Queens have died young and fair;
> Dust hath closed Helen's eye;
> I am sick, I must die—
> > *Lord, have mercy on us!*

Campion dreams of the death of his lady.

> When thou must home to shades of underground,
> And there arrived, a new admirèd guest,
> The beauteous spirits do engirt thee round,
> White Iope, blithe Helen, and the rest.

In later years, when the classical influence on our literature becomes strong again, Helen is particularly dear to Landor. Three of his longer poems dwell on her story, and her name is linked with that of his beloved Ianthe.

> Past ruin'd Ilion Helen lives,
> > Alcestis rises from the shades;
> Verse calls them forth; 'tis verse that gives
> > Immortal youth to mortal maids.

Soon shall Oblivion's deepening veil
 Hide all the peopled hills you see,
The gay, the proud, while lovers hail
 In distant ages you and me.

The tear for fading beauty check,
 For passing glory cease to sigh;
One form shall rise above the wreck,
 One name, Ianthe, shall not die.

Landor, I think, of all our earlier romantics, comes closest to the classical manner. Nor have our later poets forgotten Helen, notably Dr. Mackail, in his beautiful verses, *On the Death of Arnold Toynbee.*

Thus were the ancient days
Made like our own monotonous with grief;
 From unassuagèd lips even thus hath flown
 Perpetually the immemorial moan
Of those that weeping went on desolate ways,
 Nor found in tears relief.

For faces yet grow pale,
Tears rise at fortune, and true hearts take fire
 In all who hear, with quickening pulse's stroke,
 That cry that from the infinite people broke,
When third among them Helen led the wail
 At Hector's funeral pyre.

So long as our poetry lives, Helen will not be lost to it—"not Helen at the Skaian gate"

A second constant in poetry is the note of the nightingale. Mr. De La Mare, in the lines I have already quoted, puts it in Eden, and no doubt Eve named the bird. The ancients had a rather savage legend, Thracian, not pure Hellenic, by origin, in which King Tereus ravishes his sister-in-law Philomela, and cuts out her tongue to silence her. She reveals the secret in a piece of needlework to his sister Procne, who in revenge kills his son Itylus, and offers his flesh to the father in a dish. The gods turn Tereus into a hoopoe, Philomela into a swallow, and Procne into a nightingale. The Latin writers, such as Ovid, inverted this, and made Philomela the nightingale. So it is in Swinburne's *Itylus*, but less clearly so in that beautiful chorus from *Atalanta in Calydon*, of which I am never wearied, although elsewhere Swinburne is often capable of boring me.

> When the hounds of spring are on winter's traces,
>   The mother of months in meadow or plain
> Fills the shadows and windy places
>   With lisp of leaves and ripple of rain;
> And the brown bright nightingale amorous
> Is half assuaged for Itylus,
> For the Thracian ships and the foreign faces,
>   The tongueless vigil, and all the pain.

But the classical story does not seem to have influenced our own medieval poets of the nightingale. Chaucer, in *The Legend of Good Women*, has it briefly from Ovid, but leaves out the transformations. And before him the poets had made a fresh start with the nightingale. For them she is the singer of human love, with its ecstasies and agonies. It is so, already, in two little pieces of the late thirteenth or early fourteenth century, found in a manuscript once belonging to Leominster Abbey in Herefordshire. "Lenten is come with love to toune", one of them begins, and hails the "dayes-eyes in this dales", and the "notes suete of nyhtegales". The other is more personal in its tone.

> When the nyhtegale singes,
>   The wodes waxen grene,
> Lef aut gras ant blosme springes
>   In Aueryl, I wene;
> Ant love is to myn herte gon
>   With one spere so kene,
> Nyht and day my blod hit drynkes,
>   Myn herte deth to tene.

Secular poems of love are not very common in manuscripts of ecclesiastical origin, and I once suggested that, as the nightingale already links love and song in earlier French and Provençal literature, we might have here the reminiscences of this by some wandering English scholar on the Continent, who afterwards wrote them down among the apple-blossoms of his Herefordshire priory. But the more learned Professor Carleton Brown tells me that the poems in this manuscript are probably a collection from various sources.

Of about the same date or a little earlier is a poetical debate between *The Owl and the Nightingale*. The nightingale accuses the owl of singing about nothing but woe, while she herself rejoices. The owl replies that the nightingale's songs only encourage lust. She likes dirty perches and evil food. The nightingale defends herself. Her encouragement is all to lawful love. By the advice of the wren, the dispute is referred to the arbitration of Nicholas of Portisham in Dorset, who may be the author of the poem. Another debate, between *The Thrush and the Nightingale*, is also of the thirteenth century. The thrush denounces women; the nightingale defends them. In the fourteenth century the theme is taken up in *The Cuckoo and the Nightingale*, once ascribed to Chaucer, but now to a Sir John or Sir Thomas Clanvowe. The nightingale again upholds love, and the decision is left to a parliament to be held on St. Valentine's day. William Dunbar, in *The Merle and the Nightingale*, gives a different turn to the topic. Here the merle praises human love, but the nightingale religious love.

> All luve is lost bot vpone God allone.

Obviously, therefore, the English tradition of the nightingale, as it came down to the Renaissance, is that its song is of love. And so, of course, it is in *Romeo and Juliet*.

> Wilt thou be gone? It is not yet near day:
> It was the nightingale, and not the lark,
> That pierced the fearful hollow of thine ear;
> Nightly she sings on yon pomegranate-tree.
> Believe me, love, it was the nightingale.

But this night of love-ecstasy in Verona was only the prelude to the tragedy coming on. And it is this, perhaps, which has left later poets uncertain as to whether the note of the nightingale is really a joyous or a melancholy one. For Milton, in an early sonnet, it is "amorous", and portends success in love, but in *Il Penseroso* "most musical, most melancholy"

Coleridge, again, recorded the "pity-pleading strains" in 1795, but by 1798 had recanted.

> In Nature there is nothing melancholy.
> But some night-wandering man whose heart was pierced
> With the remembrance of a grievous wrong,
> Or slow distemper, or neglected love,
> (And so, poor wretch! filled all things with himself,
> And made all gentle sounds tell back the tale
> Of his own sorrow) he, and such as he,
> First named these notes a melancholy strain.
> And many a poet echoes the conceit.

But for himself and his friends—

> 'Tis the merry Nightingale,
> That crowds, and hurries, and precipitates
> With fast thick warble his delicious notes,
> As he were fearful that an April night
> Would be too short for him to utter forth
> His love-chant, and disburthen his full soul
> Of all its music.

Coleridge did not, however, impose his theory upon all who followed. Perhaps he was wiser when he said—

> O Lady! we receive but what we give,
> And in our life alone does Nature live:
> Ours is her wedding-garment, ours her shroud!

Wordsworth takes a line of his own. The song for him is the stock-dove's; that of the nightingale

> A song of mockery and despite
> Of shades, and dews, and silent night;
> And steady bliss, and all the loves
> Now sleeping in these peaceful groves.

It is, of course, Keats who is most conscious of the note of continuity.

> The voice I hear this passing night was heard
> In ancient days by emperor and clown:
> Perhaps the self-same song that found a path
> Through the sad heart of Ruth, when, sick for home,
> She stood in tears amid the alien corn.

There is, however, nothing about the nightingale, or any

other bird, in the *Book of Ruth*. With Christina Rossetti[1]
thinking of death, we come back to the tragic nightingale.

> I shall not see the shadows,
>   I shall not feel the rain;
> I shall not hear the nightingale
>   Sing on, as if in pain.

And it was left to a "modern" poet to follow the lead of the
thirteenth-century owl, and defame the nightingale's habits.

> The nightingales are singing near
> The Convent of the Sacred Heart,
>
> And sang within the bloody wood
> When Agamemnon cried aloud,
> And let their liquid siftings fall
> To stain the stiff dishonoured shroud.

W. B. Yeats says that these lines are written "in the grand
manner". I can only reply that they make me squirm.

This brings me to a problem about which I must say a few
words, although not very many. How far is my doctrine of
the continuity, the timelessness, of poetry applicable to
modern poetry? It is a difficult question to answer, because
we cannot see our contemporaries, as we can their predecessors, in perspective. Mr. F. L. Lucas has written an
interesting book on *The Decline and Fall of the Romantic
Ideal*. I am not clear that romanticism has fallen, although
Mr. Lucas shows that in its later stages it has sometimes
developed tendencies to neuroticism.   Yeats, although
he had a questing soul, and tried many manners, remained
at heart, I think, a romantic to the end. Byzantium is, after
all, only an outpost of Hellas. If there has been a revolt
against tradition, it has perhaps been more obvious in critical
theories about poetry than in poetry itself. The theorists
are well discussed in Sir Henry Newbolt's *A New Study of English Poetry* (1919), and again later in Mr. John Sparrow's
Sense and Poetry (1934). Here are described a number of
schools of "new" poetry, which have arisen, largely in
France and America, during the last half-century, and have
produced manifestos as to the lines on which they think that
poetry ought to be written. Symbolists, Imagists, Futurists,

Dadaists, Surrealists—they have followed each other in rapid succession. There is a good deal of the *blague* of the Paris studios about some of their utterances. But, taken as a whole, they do imply an attempt to treat the poetry of tradition as a closed account. Romance is dubbed "escapism"— not a very scholarly word-formation. "We must have done", say the Futurists, with "the dead weight of the past", with "the obsession of antiquity and Classicism". It ignores "the complete renewal of human sensibility, which has taken place since the great scientific discoveries". Life has now a quick rhythm. The poet's imagination must therefore be "a wireless imagination", an "entire freedom of images and analogies, expressed by disjointed words and without the connecting wires of syntax". And love-poetry is out of date. "The lover, pure and simple, has lost his absolute prestige." "Love has lost its absolute value." The Abbé Brémond again, a Symbolist, wanted a "pure poetry", obtaining its effects by suggestion alone, without the mediation of the intellect. It should be an experience akin to prayer, working through a mysterious quality residing in words—not in their sound, or rhythmical arrangement, still less in their intelligible content. We are far, you see, from the romantic Walter Pater's wise emphasis on the "hard logical or quasi-prosaic excellence that verse has or needs". Some echo of these exotic doctrines has drifted from overseas, and affected even English criticism, traditionally sane. A writer from one of our universities, not that to which I have the honour to belong, opines that a new technique is required, "adequate to the ways of feeling, or modes of experience, of adult, sensitive moderns". It must "develop (if at all) along some other line than that running from the Romantics, through Tennyson, Swinburne, *A Shropshire Lad*, and Rupert Brooke". And apparently it is to start from Mr. T. S. Eliot. The same pundit tells us that the first two anthologies called *Poems of To-day*, issued by this Association, "hardly contain five good poems between them". I wish he had named the four exceptions.

Frankly, I do not believe that poetry can be written in accordance with a scholastic theory, whether it is elaborated in Paris, or in Harvard, or in Cambridge. As Keats said, "If Poetry comes not as naturally as leaves to a tree, it had better not come at all". And although there have been some extravagances in modern English poetry, I do not believe that in bulk it is quite as bad as the spinners of theories would make it. "In fact," says Newbolt, "it is rare even to-day to find English poetry in which there is no trace of any meaning." There is "incoherence", but not "complete unintelligibility". I would add that even love and natural beauty are sometimes allowed to creep in. After all, men and women do still mate, although perhaps not so permanently as of old. Dawn still follows eve, and the flowers come, more or less, in their seasons. And the poets, however much they affect the manner of the wireless, cannot help being aware of these things. I am not much troubled by the fact that they are often obsessed with theories of social reorganization. A poet's politics are perhaps the least important thing about him. The chief defect, I think, lies in an imperfect feeling for rhythm. Free verse is no novelty. Milton used it in its rhymed form, and Arnold in its unrhymed. But it requires a strong sense of rhythm to do without the incantation which a recurrent stanza-form brings.

In conclusion, I will emphasize my own impression of the timelessness, the continuity, of poetry, by reading the two pieces which have most affected me recently, when I came across them for the first time. One is a late fifteenth-century poem, in which the word-terminations have rather broken down. It is a movement, the *Gloria in Excelsis*, from *The Lover's Mass*.

> Worshyppe to that lord above,
> That callyd ys the god of love,
> Pes to hys seruantes euerychon,
> Trewe of herte, stable as ston,
> > That feythful be.
>
> To hertys trewe of ther corage,
> That lyst chaunge for no rage,
> But kep hem in ther hestys stylle,
> In all maner wedris ylle,
> > Pes, concord and vnyte.

God send hem sone ther desyrs
And reles of ther hoote ffyrs
That brenneth at her herte sore,
And encresseth more and more,
   This my prayere.

And after wynter wyth hys shourys
God send hem counfort of may flourys,
Affter gret wynd and stormys kene,
The glade sonne with bemys shene
   May appere,

To yive hem lyght affter dyrknesse,
Joye eke after hevynesse;
And after dool and ther wepynge,
To here the somer foullys synge,
   God yive grace.

For ofte sythe men ha seyn
A ful bryght day after gret reyn,
And tyl the storme be leyd asyde,
The herdys vnder bussh abyde,
   And taketh place.

After also the dirke nyght,
Voyde off the Mone and sterre lyght,
And after nyghtys dool and sorowe,
Folweth ofte a ful glade morowe
   Of Auenture.

Now lorde, that knowest hertys alle
Off louers that for helpe calle,
On her trouthe of mercy rewe,
Namly on swyche as be trewe.
   Helpe to recure.
   Amen.

The other is Mr. Hilaire Belloc's *Ha'nacker Mill*.[1]

Sally is gone that was so kindly,
Sally is gone from Ha'nacker Hill.
 And the Briar grows ever since then so blindly
 And ever since then the clapper is still,
 And the sweeps have fallen from Ha'nacker Mill

[1] From *Sonnets and Verse* (1938 Edn.), Gerald Duckworth & Co., Ltd.

Ha'nacker Hill is in Desolation:
　　Ruin a-top and a field unploughed.
And Spirits that call on a fallen nation
　　Spirits that loved her calling aloud:
　　Spirits abroad in a windy cloud.

Spirits that call and no one answers;
　　Ha'nacker's down and England's done.
Wind and Thistle for pipe and dancers
　　And never a ploughman under the Sun.
　　Never a ploughman. Never a one.

Nearly five centuries divide these two poems, but both, when I first read them, gave me the same authentic thrill, although I do not know that my physical reactions were exactly the same as A. E. Housman's.

8th June, 1940.

THE DEDICATED LIFE

AMONG the enduring legacies of the Greek spirit to the consolation and refreshment of man are those little sets of verses, generally from four to eight lines long, which are known as the Epigrams. In the grace of their structure and the finish of their details, they stand to the greater writings of the Attic poets, as do the exquisite figurines of Tanagra to the monumental conceptions of Phidias or Praxiteles. An epigram is literally an inscription, something written on something else, and a few of the Greek epigrams have in fact come down to us in graven form. An epigram is therefore naturally short, and has a relation to the object upon which it is written. It is a comment, a reflection. And when epigrams cease to be inscribed and become literary exercises, although their range is widened, they often retain traces of their origin. There is the play of the imagination around some concrete object: a shrine, a tomb, a lintel, a work of art, a gift. The writing of the extant Greek epigrams began in the seventh century B.C. and lasted well into the Middle Ages. It is "startling", as Dr. Mackail points out, to think that they overlapped the *Divine Comedy* and the beginnings of our own vernacular poetry.[1] But of course the later, Byzantine, examples follow an inherited convention. The best epigrams are of the sixth century B.C., and the art was still vital during its classic and Alexandrine successors. The basis of what we have was a collection ascribed to Meleager in the first century. It is called a "crown" or "garland". We should call it an "anthology".

The range of the epigrams is no narrower than that of life itself. They tell of the tender things of love and death, of homespun family incidents, of labour and revel, of striking events, of the marvels of nature and of craft. They give imperishable form to the wise maxims of a garnered experience. They play on the surface of the human comedy. A

---

[1] J. W. Mackail, *Select Epigrams from the Greek Anthology*, 8. I have made free use of Dr. Mackail's translations.

large group of them, to which I want more particularly to direct your attention, are dedications. In these the fundamental conception of the epigram as an inscription is still dominant. They accompany gifts to the gods. You may readily think of them as placed on some domestic or wayside shrine. The husbandman has come upon a cool well-spring in the heat of noon and lays his offering on a slab of rock. "And may ye fare well, O Nymphs, and may your lovely feet tread this house of waters while ye fill it with a pure draught." Or there has been a good harvest, although from a stony soil, and here is a cake "for Demeter of the winnowing-fan and the Seasons whose feet are in the furrows". The woodman brings a walking-staff of wild olive cut with his bill-hook for Herakles, the maker of songs a bunch of dew-sprent roses and thyme for the maidens of Helicon. Apollo must have the hunter's lucky bow, and to make it the more acceptable, he has bound it with rings of gold. The fishermen catch a shoal of tunny with their nets of hemp in the green sea-ways, and Priapus of the Shore gets a stool of heather and a cup, that he may rest and be refreshed after the dance. Or they may carry some marvel of the beach, or merely bread and wine and a broiled red mullet and a hake, asking the recompense of brimming nets, for "to thee, O blessed one, all meshes have been given". The seaman at outsetting brings his libation and "the gleam of a brief-shining lamp", and prays for a favourable breeze. On his return, he has with him a model of his ship. It has been tossed with the wandering winds, and he has been in fear of death, but now his foot is secure on earth. The land traveller has nothing but his hat to lay before Artemis of the Ways. "It is a small thank-offering, but from a holy heart." These are the simple gifts of simple folk, but at the beginning and end of every enterprise an observance is right. And what is for the gods is often the utensil of some occupation now laid aside, with relief or with regret, or with that mingling of the two which often accompanies such turns of life. Archestratus, the spent warrior, dedicates his shield to Herakles; Telesilla, on her marriage one supposes, the instruments of her industry to the Mistress of wool-dressers, spindle and bobbins and basket, and "the shuttle that sang at morning with the earliest swallows' cry, the kingfisher of Pallas's loom"; Lais, the lady of many lovers, her mirror to Aphrodite, "for I cannot see myself as I was, and as I am, I will not."

Obviously the epigrams have passed through the crucible of the poetic imagination. But, as obviously, they reflect elements that had a real existence in the life from which their materials were drawn. And they give us a different picture of pagan religion from that which we get through the spectacles of early Christian controversialists. Here are none of the "vain imaginings of the heathen"—those grotesque or indecent adventures which the temple-attendants attributed to their gods, in an attempt to explain ancient features of ritual, the origin of which was forgotten. Nor have we quite that ordered hierarchy of departmentalized deities, which was the conception of a more sophisticated and speculative theology. The living polytheism of Greece rested on a vague general sense or a power of powers, outside and beyond man, which if rightly approached might be friendly to him, and if not, hostile; of something—

> deeply interfused,
> Whose dwelling is the light of setting suns,
> And the round ocean and the living air,
> And the blue sky, and in the mind of man. [1]

Largely it is one power, under various aspects. Artemis is the lady of the woods, but also the lady of the ways and the lady of the havens, the patroness of all who pursue their avocations beneath the visiting moon. A lover, starting to fetch his bride from across the Aegean, prays to Aphrodite, as the mistress at once of the wedding chamber and of seafaring. These are homely divinities, gods of all work. And the way of approach to them is through dedication. Anthropologists may trace the practice of dedication to earlier ways of thought, in which the divinity is hardly distinguishable from the thing dedicated or that again from him who dedicates. But, at the stage to which the epigrams belong, a dedication is clearly a gift. Something is due, even from

---

[1] Wordsworth's *Lines on Tintern Abbey.*

poverty, to the power which gives all things, and the rendering of it is linked to the best moments of man's life, to his uprising and his downsitting, to the hopefulness of morning and the sense of rest at eve or in old age. And so we get one step further, for what is due is not an external gift alone; it is something also in the behaviour and the heart of man himself. "He who enters the incense-filled temple must be holy, and holiness is to have a pure mind", says an epigram. The Roman conception of *pietas* gives us much the same double sense, of accustomed recognition and uprightness of purpose.

This religious background, even if modified in city surroundings, makes it easy to understand the preoccupation of Greek philosophy with spiritual values, the constant antithesis of τὸ ζῆν and τὸ εὖ ζῆν, of life merely lived and life as it should be lived. Our own ethical attitude owes so much to the fervour of the Jewish prophets for righteousness, that we sometimes tend to overlook the contribution of the Greeks in exploring the *content* of righteousness, in the analysis of the virtues and the graces, as well as in stressing those elements of the good life, the pursuit of truth, and the pursuit of beauty, which are remote from Jewish thought. But even for the Greeks righteousness came first, and it is "startling" again to read a sentence so modern in its altruism as that of the comic poet Menander:—

This is life, not to live for oneself alone.[1]

And when Greek philosophy reaches its culminating point, to many minds, in the writings of Plato, we get at last the notion, not merely of the dedication of what is due from all men, but of the dedication of life itself. It is in that amazing dream of the *Republic*, where Socrates, puzzled in explaining to his pupils the nature of Righteousness, the principle of order and balance among the powers and instincts of man, falls back upon an analogy from the constitution of the ideal state. Here, he says, there must be three classes, each fulfilling in completeness its own proper function: a class of artisans and traders, fashioning perfect products of handicraft, buying and selling perfectly; above them a class of

[1] *Fragm. incert.*, 257, τοῦτ᾽ ἔστι τὸ ζῆν οὐχ ἑαυτῷ ζῆν μόνον.

warriors, wardens of the state, perfect in their swordsman-
ship; above these again a class of rulers, wardens in a fuller
sense, perfect in the art of government. Righteousness in
the state means the exercise by each class of its own peculiar
virtue, without intermeddling in that of any other, and in due
subordination to the rulers. He goes at some length into the
education of the wardens, especially the rulers, and he pre-
scribes for them an austere, and to the plain mind a paradoxical, rule of life. They are to seek none of the profits and
advantages which ordinary rulers claim; to live simply, to
own no personal property, to have not even wives and
children of their own, "for among friends all things should
be in common". Even their houses are to be free of access
to all citizens. And in these houses no gold is to be seen,
since rulers have gold in their souls, where other men have
only silver or brass. In all things, those who are to be the
masters of the state must be as its servants. Then the pupils
break in. "It is beautiful, Socrates, but how on earth is it
to be brought about?" And Socrates is driven to his familiar
irony. "You must not press me too hard. I am one of those
idle fellows who like to work out the logical implications of
an idea which strikes them, without stopping to enquire too
closely into its feasibility. And yet, might it not come true,
on one condition, that either philosophers should be made
kings, or kings should become philosophers?" Of course,
it is all a dream, a Cloud Cuckoo Land, as Aristophanes will
point out. There never were such wardens, and there never
will be such wardens. No philosopher is going to be made
king, and if he were, he would not long remain one. It would
be "roses, roses, all the way", as Browning puts it, at the
beginning of the year, and at the end the cup of hemlock.
Plato does not take it too seriously. After all, he is mainly
aiming at his analogy with the individual character, in which
the appetites, like the trading folk, should be in subjection,
the passions and the will should be the trained warriors, while
the ordering of the whole should be for the philosophic
mind, capable of conceiving the Good. And yet, even in the
political sphere, he does mean a good deal of it, thinking that
the true statesman should rule, not for himself but for others,

with a constant abnegation of merely personal ambitions and desires, living, so far as man may, the dedicated life.

It has often been pointed out that the nearest approach to the paradox of the philosopher-king is in the stoical Marcus Aurelius, musing to himself on the lonely eminence of his throne, in the consciousness of the burden of empire, and of the obligation to make no demands for himself, but to refer all things to the law of service.

This is the way of salvation—to look thoroughly into everything and see what it really is, alike in matter and in cause; with your whole heart to do what is just and say what is true; and one thing more, to find life's fruition in heaping good on good so close that not a chink is left between.[1]

History has, no doubt, its other approximations. They are no more, and I shall not pursue them. Nor shall I dwell at length upon the dedicated life, as it appears, on a grand scale, in the Christian scheme of things. This is too large, and perhaps too controversial a topic, for a desultory lecture. The priesthood belongs to the Judaic rather than the Hellenic element in Christianity. In the traditional religion of Greece, as the epigrams represent it, priests performed certain ritual acts, but they were not the ministers of worship, or the appointed teachers of righteousness. Approach to the divine powers was normally for the head of each family at his hearth, or for the magistrate at the greater hearth of the city. Even on the Judaic side, it is the prophet rather than the priest who is the prototype. And it is to be noted that in the Christian philosophy the setting apart of the priest is a matter of vocation, rather than of dedication as an act of individual will. If I may take Dr. Gore as an exponent of that philosophy in its sacramental aspect, the primary agent, in ordination, as in the process of redemption itself, is the Holy Spirit. Priesthood is a gift of God, which is on a man through the sacramental channel of the laying on of hands.[2] The earlier offices of ordination do not in fact include any formula of self-dedication by the candidate; that of the Anglican church

[1] Trans. G. H. Rendall, xii, 29.
[2] C. Gore, *The Holy Spirit and the Church*, 7.

does, by way of question and answer. And before entry into
the more completely dedicated life of the monastic orders
there were of course definite vows and symbolical cere-
monies of renunciation. I do not want to make too much of
the distinction between vocation and dedication. Dr. Gore
does not believe that sacraments are "charms which could be
beneficial without moral response". The gift of the Holy
Spirit must be followed by an act of will; of will, not merely
of emotion; Dr. Gore distrusts emotion. The dedicated life
of priests and monks and friars has been a great force in the
moulding of civilization. But it must be recognized that the
setting aside has not always been followed by the act of will,
and that the act of will has not always proved enduring. The
history of monachism is one of a constant succession of new
rules and new orders in the endeavour for reformation. Plato
would have approved the spirit of the vows, but might have
noted with irony how much of the land of England, at the
end of the Middle Ages, was in the possession of com-
munities vowed to poverty.

And now, since righteousness, although the chief of the
spiritual values, is not the only one, I will turn to the dedicated life of poets. Poetry in its essence is the outcome of an
emotional reaction to experiences and activities which are
themselves distinct from poetry. It has often been used as a
means of living. But the notion of poetry as an end of life
starts, I believe, so far as English literature is concerned,
with the humanism of the sixteenth century. And probably
it owes much to the great example of Vergil. Vergil, a man of
frail health, and with means assured by his relation to the
court of Octavius, did in fact spend his life in the composition of poetry. The *Georgics* took him seven years, and
the *Aeneid*, which he had in mind from the beginning, was
still uncompleted when he died at the age of fifty-one. He
planned it and re-planned it, and wrote it and re-wrote it.
On his death-bed he begged that it might be destroyed as
imperfect, but this was not done. It had long been in expectation, not merely in the words of Propertius, as "something
greater than the Iliad", but as a contribution to that re-
modelling of the Roman polity, and with it the whole of

western civilization, in which Octavius was engaged. The Emperor himself deigned to watch its fortunes. Vergil has been the model, consciously or unconsciously, for the writers of most of the greater poems conceived in the spirit of humanism; consciously enough for Dante, and in our own tongue, for Spenser and for Milton. It is in Milton that the conception of a life dedicated to poetry can first be closely studied. He, too, was of weak health, which ultimately led to blindness, and of sufficient means. And, like Vergil, he had been trained in all the learning of his age. A fortunate turn for autobiographical reference enables us to trace fairly clearly the history and outcome of his deliberate resolve. We do not know when he formed it. The poems and letters of his early life for the most part reflect the contemplation of the scholar rather than the dawn of a creative impulse. But there is a first note of what was to come in the sonnet which he wrote on the eve of his departure from Cambridge:

> How soon hath Time, the subtle thief of youth,
> Stol'n on his wing my three and twenti'th year!
> My hasting days fly on with full career,
> But my late spring no bud or blossom shew'th.
>
> Yet be it less or more, or soon or slow,
> It shall be still in strictest measure ev'n,
> To that same lot, however mean, or high,
> Toward which Time leads me, and the will of Heav'n;
> All is, if I have grace to use it so,
> As ever in my great task Master's eye.

Shortly afterwards, now back in his father's house at Horton for six more years of studious retirement, he put a copy of this sonnet into a letter and sent it to a friend as part of an apology for his life "as yet obscure and unserviceable to mankind". It is not, as the friend thinks, to "the endless delight of speculation" that "this my tardy moving" is due, but to "a sacred reverence and religious advisement how best to undergo, not taking thought of being late, so it give advantage to be more fit". Yet, he adds, "I am something suspicious of myself, and do take notice of a certain belatedness in me", and therefore he sends the sonnet.[1] And still

[1] *Trinity College, Cambridge, MS.*, f. 6.

the task of preparation went on. Some years later he writes in Latin to another friend, or perhaps the same:

You ask what I am thinking of? So may the good Deity help me, of immortality! And what am I doing? Growing my wings and meditating flight; but as yet our Pegasus raises himself on very tender pinions. Let us be lowly wise![1]

Here the language already suggests an endeavour in poetry, and this became a fixed intention during a visit to Italy at the age of thirty, when, as Milton records, he was encouraged by the praises of its academies, and—

began thus far to assent both to them and divers of my friends here at home, and not less to an inward prompting which now grew daily upon me, that by labour and intense study (which I take to be my portion in this life), joined with the strong propensity of nature, I might perhaps leave something so written to aftertimes, as they should not willingly let it die.[2]

Other references from the Italian period show that what Milton first had in mind was a poem on British history and in particular on Arthur and his Round Table. But it is not likely that he wrote anything of this. When he came home, he set up his staff in London as a teacher. And here a mind, to which after all the serious things of life appealed from more than one angle, became involved in all the political and religious problems of that most controversial age. The poem that he should have written of Arthur turned to pamphlets in defence of liberty—liberty in church order, liberty in printing, liberty from despotism, and, after an unfortunate personal experience, liberty in the marriage tie. It ended in the appointment as Latin Secretary to the Council of State, and in the long defences of republican politics, which cost Milton his eyesight.

> What supports me, dost thou ask?
> The conscience, Friend, to have lost them overply'd
> In liberty's defence, my noble task,
> Of which all Europe talks from side to side.[3]

[1] *Familiar Letters*, vii.
[2] *Reason of Church Government.*   [3] *Sonnet to Cyriack Skinner.*

Liberty, you see, has now become Milton's "task". Meanwhile, the great poem is unwritten; unwritten, but never forgotten. The earlier pamphlets, at least, are full of aspirations towards it. When the forces of Antichrist are broken:—

Then, amidst the hymns and hallelujahs of saints, some one may perhaps be heard offering at high strains in new and lofty measures, to sing and celebrate thy divine mercies and marvellous judgments in this land throughout all ages.[1]

One tract, in particular, contains a long passage of musing on what might be done "of highest hope and hardest attempting", on whether the epic or the dramatic form would be preferable, on "what king or knight, before the conquest, might be chosen in whom to lay the pattern of a Christian hero". It is a reluctant anticipation of "the thing which I had to say and those intentions which have lived within me ever since I could conceive myself anything worth to my country". But it must still be for the future, when the land is freed from "this impertinent yoke of prelaty, under whose inquisitorious and tyrannical duncery no free and splendid wit can flourish". Then comes Milton's magnificent avowal of the nature of poetic inspiration, as he conceives it.

Neither do I think it shame to covenant with any knowing reader, that for some years yet I may go on trust with him toward the payment of what I am now indebted, as being a work not to be raised from the heat of youth, or the vapours of wine; like that which flows at waste from the pen of some vulgar amorist, or the trencher fury of a rhyming parasite; nor to be obtained by the invocation of Dame Memory and her Siren daughters, but by devout prayer to that eternal Spirit, who can enrich with all utterance and knowledge, and send out his seraphim, with the hallowed fire of his altar, to touch and purify the lips of whom he pleases.[2]

Poetic dedication, thus stated, becomes indistinguishable from religious vocation. To the same period belong those jottings on possible themes for literary composition, which

---

[1] *Of Reformation in England;* cf. *Animadversions upon the Remonstrant's Defence.*
[2] *The Reason of Church Government.*

are still preserved in Milton's handwriting at Trinity College,
Cambridge. They include lists of episodes from British and
Scottish history. One is of Macbeth. "An heroicall Poem",
notes Milton, "may be founded somewhere in Alfred's reign,
especially at his issuing out of Edelingsey on the Danes,
whose actions are well like those of Ulysses." But Arthur has
now passed out of sight, and for the most part Milton's
imagination is turning around scriptural subjects, and shaping
them for tragedy in the classical manner, rather than for
epic. An *Abraham*, a *Baptistes*, a *Samson*, are among the titles.
But there is already more than one elaborate *scenario* for a
Paradise Lost. Possibly some attempt at a beginning of this
may have been made. John Aubrey tells us that Milton's
nephew, Edward Phillips, pointed out to him half-a-dozen
verses in the poem as we know it, and said that they were
written fifteen or sixteen years before the rest, and for a
tragedy.[1] However this may be, it was not before his fiftieth
year that Milton, blind, worn with battles, perhaps already
catching sound of the advancing trumpets of the Restoration,
sat down to accomplish the task which he had set himself in
the sylvan shades of Horton or among the cultured academies
of Italy. *Paradise Lost* has its own autobiographical reminiscences.

> Thee I re-visit now with bolder wing,
> Escap't the *Stygian* Pool, though long detain'd
> In that obscure sojourn, while in my flight
> Through utter and through middle darkness borne
> With other notes then to th' *Orphean* lyre
> I sung of *Chaos* and *Eternal Night*.[2]

The dream of Arthur is recalled. Milton will not now sing
of

> fabl'd Knights
> In Battels feign'd.

He has a "higher argument"—

> If answerable style I can obtaine
> Of my Celestial Patroness, who deignes
> Her nightly visitation unimplor'd,

[1] J. Aubrey, *Brief Lives*, ii, 69.   [2] *P.L.* iii, 13.

> And dictates to me slumbring, or inspires
> Easie my unpremeditated Verse:
> Since first this Subject for Heroic Song
> Pleas'd me long choosing, and beginning late.[1]

I shall have another word to say of Milton later. But for the moment I pass over the eighteenth century, which yielded no *Paradise Lost*, but fixed by its terminology the notion of the Poet, or the Bard, as in some sort a particular species of man. And I come to the nearest counterpart of Milton's spiritual self-dedication, in that of Wordsworth. Here again we get help from autobiography, in the retrospect of the *Prelude*, now recovered for us in its earlier and psychologically its most interesting form by the devoted labours of Profesor De Selincourt. Perhaps a first moment of initiation is fixed by Wordsworth himself. It was during a Cambridge vacation, after a night of village "dancing, gaiety and mirth", and "young love-liking", on a walk homeward at daybreak.

> Magnificent
> The morning was, in memorable pomp,
> More glorious than I ever had beheld.
> The Sea was laughing at a distance; all
> The solid Mountains were as bright as clouds,
> Grain-tinctured, drench'd in empyrean light;
> And, in the meadows and the lower grounds,
> Was all the sweetness of a common dawn,
> Dews, vapours, and the melody of birds,
> And Labourers going forth into the fields.
> —Ah! need I say, dear Friend, that to the brim
> My heart was full; I made no vows, but vows
> Were then made for me; bond unknown to me
> Was given, that I should be, else sinning greatly,
> A dedicated Spirit. On I walk'd
> In blessedness, which even yet remains.[2]

The expression is somewhat mystical, and one must remember that, while Wordsworth's memory of natural sights and sounds was retentive, some projection backwards of a later self may colour the statements in the *Prelude* of his spiritual reactions to these. He does not tell us when this

[1] *P.L.,* ix, 20.   [2] *Prelude,* iv, 330.

sense of dedication became explicit. But it is implied in much of the narrative that follows. In 1792 he spent a year in France amid the Revolution; a stormy period, both in its internal and its external experience. Had he not been recalled by lack of funds, he tells Coleridge:—

> I doubtless should have made a common cause
> With some who perish'd, haply perish'd, too,
> A poor mistaken and bewilder'd offering,
> Should to the breast of Nature have gone back
> With all my resolutions, all my hopes,
> A Poet only to myself, to Men
> Useless, and even, beloved Friend! a soul
> To thee unknown.[1]

Back in England, distressed, unsettled, moving rather aimlessly, it would seem, between town and country, he has strong convictions, notably on a lonely journey over Salisbury Plain, of the place of poets in the scheme of things, and for himself:—

> that in some sort I possess'd
> A privilege, and that a work of mine,
> Proceeding from the depth of untaught things,
> Enduring and creative, might become
> A power like one of Nature's.[2]

Wordsworth's vague purpose took a more definite shape, under the joint stimulus of Coleridge and of his own sister Dorothy, soon after he had settled down, at the age of twenty-five, to a life of seclusion, rarely interrupted in later years. It was Coleridge who suggested to him, as they paced the quiet coombes of Nether Stowey, a great philosophical poem, to be called *The Recluse*, or *Views on Man, Nature and Society*. A start was made, but Wordsworth soon fell into a mood of depression, which also he records at the beginning of the *Prelude*.

> But I have been discouraged; gleams of light
> Flash often from the East, then disappear
> And mock me with a sky that ripens not
> Into a steady morning: if my mind,

---

[1] *Prelude*, x, 195.   [2] *Prelude*, xii, 308.

> Remembering the sweet promise of the past,
> Would gladly grapple with some noble theme,
> Vain is her wish; where'er she turns she finds
> Impediments from day to day renew'd.

He believes that he has "that first great gift, the vital soul", and store both of "general truths" and of "external things, forms, images". But he is unable to make "steady choice" of a subject, now contemplating a subject from British chronicle,

> some old
> Romantic tale, by Milton left unsung;

now one of chivalry and pastoral, or of history, Mithridates or Sertorius or Gustavus Adolphus or the like. The conscious reminiscence of Milton's own hesitations is obvious.

> Then, last wish,
> My last and favourite aspiration! then
> I yearn towards some philosophic Song
> Of Truth that cherishes our daily life;
> With meditations passionate from deep
> Recesses in man's heart, immortal verse
> Thoughtfully fitted to the Orphean lyre;
> But from this awful burthen I full soon
> Take refuge, and beguile myself with trust
> That mellower years will bring a riper mind
> And clearer insight.

And so he is, he fears

> Unprofitably travelling towards the grave,
> Like a false steward who hath much received,
> And renders nothing back.[1]

It was perhaps at this time that Wordsworth found his "refuge" in planning and addressing to Coleridge, as an introduction to the *Recluse*, the poem on the growth of his own mind, which became the *Prelude*. Here philosophy could be approached, not directly, but as a comment upon narrative. If a beginning was in fact made with the *Prelude* at Nether Stowey, it was soon laid aside for the *Lyrical Ballads*. It was taken up during a visit to Germany in 1799, but dropped again in the following year, when the impulse of Grasmere made the *Recluse* once more seem possible. Then both enter-

[1] *Prelude*, i, 134-271.

prises passed together into the background. The early years
at Grasmere were a period of great productivity, but almost
entirely in poems of shorter inspiration. The *Prelude* was
resumed and finished in 1804 and 1805. The *Recluse* was
never finished. It was, in its final conception, to have three
parts. The first and third were to be meditations in the
author's own person, the second to take a more dramatic
form. The second part appeared alone, as the *Excursion*, in
1814. One book of the first part also exists. The *Prelude* was
not printed until after Wordsworth's death. It is evident
from the family correspondence that the completion of the
Recluse was long hoped for, but in vain. "He has not looked
at it", writes Dorothy in 1821: "He will never govern his
labours." She has the same tale to tell in 1824. And so it
passes into oblivion.

Two reflections are suggested by this poetic history. One
is, that Coleridge was clearly wrong in thinking that Wordsworth could write a philosophic poem, if indeed a philosophic
poem is possible at all. Wordsworth's imagination had not
the continuous flow of Milton's, whose muse inspired "easie
my unpremeditated verse", once the great structure was
planned. It was intense, but slow to move, much depending
on recurrent impulses from external things or the memory of
them—"emotion recollected in tranquillity". The actual
process of composition was difficult to him, difficult and ex-
hausting. Dorothy's journals record his wrestlings, day by
day, over the revision even of small poems. The ample
Miltonic sweep over an abstract theme was not for him. In
the *Prelude* he had his vivid sense of the past to fall back upon.
Secondly, the analogy between Wordsworth's career and
that of Milton, so close in some ways at first, does not endure.
Critics have differed as to the effect of Milton's controversial
life upon his ultimate achievement. But for politics and war,
suggests Professor Grierson, we might have had "a finer
union in his great poem of the humanist temper of the Greeks
with the spirituality of the Hebrew prophets".[1] It may be so,
but it is also possible to hold that it was the life in contact
with humanity which gave him the material out of which to

[1] *Cross Currents in English Literature of the Seventeenth Century*, 280.

build his lofty fabrics. Wordsworth set out to write of Man,
Nature, and Society. He never lost contact with nature. With·
society he largely did, after his seclusion began. I do not
mean that he ceased to take interest in public affairs, but
that his interest was that of a spectator *ab extra*, not a parti-
cipant. And even with men, as individuals, his most deter-
mining relations, outside his own family, and for a time
Coleridge, remained those of his boyhood. To the Grasmere yeomen and peasants he stood as a being remote and
inscrutable. It was Hartley Coleridge who talked and drank
with them. And so, detached and unrefreshed, Wordsworth's poetic impulses flagged and failed before half his
days were spent. It was only while the dew of his early
dedication was still on him that he became, in Matthew
Arnold's words,—

> A priest to us all
> Of the wonder and bloom of the world,
> Which we saw with his eyes, and were glad.[1]

Am I representing life-long poetic dedication as a mirage?
Perhaps it is, if it becomes an attempt at a continuous
emotional response to activities which are not lived, but only
observed. After all, how much of our best poetry has been
written by men whose main occupation was not poetry. One
thinks of Chaucer, toiling at his bills of lading, of Shakespeare, decorating with poetry his primary task of amusing a
rough audience with jests and exciting it with violence, of
Matthew Arnold himself—well, I suppose that school-
inspecting is an activity.

I have one point more, with which, when I began this dis-
quisition, I meant to deal more fully. But the pen of an un-
practised lecturer runs away with him. It concerns not
poetry alone, but all forms of the dedicated life, whatever its
objective; altruistic service, the production of beauty, the
disinterested search for truth. How far can any life be completely a dedicated one?

> Give all thou canst; high Heaven rejects the lore
> Of nicely-calculated less or more,[2]

says Wordsworth, and no doubt in some sort of sense that is

---

[1] *The Youth of Nature.*   [2] *Sonnet on King's College Chapel.*

true.　But modern social philosophy teaches us, I suppose, that man on earth is under an economic necessity to earn his bread by labour, and that from a biological point of view the pursuit of spiritual values is to be regarded as a kind of play, the overflow of surplus energies, exercising themselves freely when the economic necessity has been satisfied. And a modern ethical sense does not accept, so readily as that of the past, some at least of the economic devices by which the dedicated life has been maintained.　It is offended if a poet lives by patronage or in the enjoyment of a sinecure. Even of Wordsworth we should have thought better if he had executed his office of a stamp-distributor personally, and not through a lowly-paid deputy.　Perhaps we have not yet reached the point when it becomes a reproach to a man that he lives upon the inherited wealth of the past, but will the development of the social conscience stop short of that?　From a second angle, therefore, we seem to be brought to the conclusion that the dedicated life must in some way reconcile its spiritual ends with others more mundane.　How is the balance to be established?　The dilemma is sharpest for the poet, since poetry is not marketable, except at the risk of ceasing to be poetry.　Perhaps the solution for him lies in acceptance of the view that poetry is not the substance of human living, but the response to living in moments of emotion.　About the poet, however, I have said enough.　I come back to Plato and his wardens, whom I take leave to regard as represented in our day by the great body of public servants, and not least by those who, like many to whom I speak, are bound to the service of education.　They, too, have a spiritual value to uphold and it asks for dedication. Let me recall the emotional response of one who stood high among them—

> I vow to thee, my country—all earthly things above—
> Entire and whole and perfect, the service of my love,
> The love that asks no questions: the love that stands the test,
> That lays upon the altar the dearest and the best:
> The love that never falters, the love that pays the price,
> The love that makes undaunted the final sacrifice.[1]

[1] Sir Cecil Spring-Rice, *Collected Poems*.

We live in a time when the pressure of economic necessity is stern. It is bringing with it, if I may again quote Wordsworth, much "pillage of man's ancient heart."[1] Even education, says a glib maker of phrases, "must be mobilised behind industry and commerce". I hope that it is not quite so bad as all that. But clearly there is all the more and not the less call, if the spiritual values are to be maintained, for the disinterested activities of public servants. And they, too, cannot evade the biological problem. Even Plato recognised that the wardens must live at the expense of the State. But it was to be a spare life. We need not follow the paradoxical austerity which denied to the wardens the use of gold and the human joys of wife and family. Nevertheless, even in sober mood, Plato would have held that the dedicated life must be, comparatively, a spare one.

1931.

[1] *Sonnet to Sarah Hutchinson.*

GHOSTS IN THE BODLEIAN

WE ARE the Friends of the Bodleian, and the report which I hold, with its long chronicle of stone after stone added to that historic cairn, tells me that we have been so for just ten years. But to many of us the Bodleian itself has been the dearest of friends during most of a lifetime; the nursing mother of our earliest attempts at independent study; to some a daily companion, to others a *refrigerium* for the spirit, when in the stress of less congenial labours else-where we recalled, as I find myself writing over thirty years ago, those quiet corridors, where scholars sit from morn to eve, disturbed only by the green flicker of leaves in the Exeter garden, or the statutory inconvenience of a terminal lecture. We were told, quite recently, by a very good friend of the Bodleian, that the coming development of University Educa-tion in England would lie with institutions other than Oxford and Cambridge. It may be so. I am no competitor in the dangerous art of vaticination, and am quite ready to believe the worst of the future. But when I enter the great quad-rangle which is to be the ultimate fortress of the doomed humanities, I sometimes remember that prophecy, and re-member also the whimsical outburst of Charles Lamb upon a slighter provocation, "Very well; I will write for antiquity" Impatient modernism once suggested that the old Bodleian should be left to its ghosts, and a new one built in some wilderness. That menace has passed, but I often fancy that I should like to see those ghosts. Some evening perhaps, when Bodley's bell rings, one might elude the vigilance of librar-ians and janitor, and conceal oneself, to await their coming. I should not know all of that goodly company, but there are some for whom I should keep a special watch. And the first would be that eponymous hero whose fame has been rather overshadowed by that of Bodley himself. Humphrey, Duke of Gloucester, was long in the front of English politics, although he came to a bitter end. But history knows him best as the chief counterpart over here of the cultivated Italian princes of the Renaissance. Books, and especially classical books, were the passion of his later life. One Italian scholar translated for him the *Ethics* and *Politics* of Aristotle, another the *Republic* of Plato; just the books which have so long been the foundation of Oxford philosophy. He read the books. Those of Plato, in particular, he read and re-read. They should be, he says, "counsellors and companions for so much of our life as is left to us". It is a pleasing detail that he called his daughter Antigone, after the *Thebais* of Seneca, I suppose, since he certainly knew nothing of the Greek tragedians. He had Petrarch, too, and Boccaccio, and Dante, apparently in the original. One minor humanist, Tito Livio Frulovisi of Ferrara, formerly a schoolmaster in Venice, he invited to England, and there Frulovisi wrote for him a Latin life of Henry V, of which incidentally a better text than Hearne's is much to be desired. It is possible that Humphrey has also a place in the history of the stage in this country, for a learned Cambridge scholar, Dr. Previté-Orton, has recently edited a number of Latin comedies by Frulovisi, two of which he thinks, although I am not quite sure that he is right, were written for the Duke. If so, they may have been performed in his "Manor of Pleasance", which became Greenwich Palace.

Of Oxford, Humphrey was the accepted patron—*literatissimus princeps, amicissimus noster*—and to Oxford he gave most of his books. They were lodged in the old book-room built by Bishop Cobham behind St. Mary's, and here by 1445 the crowd around the lecterns became so great that the University wrote to Humphrey, suggesting a new library, in a place fairly remote from secular din, where a new school was in building. This was the Divinity School where we are gathered, to the funds for which Humphrey had already contributed. The library was, no doubt, to be, as it is, a second story, and of this they offered Humphrey the *titulum fundacionis*. Humphrey responded by a promise of £100 and the rest of his Latin books. But two years later came his death, perhaps his murder, and a long string of letters to Henry VI and his courtiers failed to get the promise redeemed. Henry is indeed suspected of diverting the books to his own foundation of King's College, Cambridge. The library was, however, built with the help of a thousand marks from Thomas Kempe, Bishop of London, to whom an oblivious University wrote of *tuam novam librariam*. Humphrey, it will be seen, can never have set foot during his lifetime in the room which bears his name, but it may reasonably be assumed that, in view of that *titulum fundacionis*, his ghost may claim what is called the right of free access. But when I see him, that princely countenance will be perturbed. Humphrey will be moving uneasily from shelf to shelf, looking at the titles of the volumes. "Where are my books?", he mutters. "Two hundred and eighty-one noble books I gave them, and I can only find two, and what seems to be a copy of a third. Where is the Plato I loved; my Plutarch, my Demosthenes, my Cicero, my Terence, my Ovid? What have they done with them?" I shall not be able to tell him, and I do not believe that any one else will. Tradition, through the mouth of Anthony Wood, ascribes a rifling of Oxford libraries to the Edwardian commissioners in 1550 and in particular to Richard Cox, then Chancellor. Manuscripts guilty of no other superstition than red letters in their fronts or titles were destroyed. Books of divinity were carried on biers as a funeral of Scotus and the Scotists, and given to mechanicals. Wood had heard it credibly reported from ancient men, and they while young from scholars of great standing, that some copies of the Greek Testament hardly escaped. He is sure that books with angles or mathematical diagrams were treated as Papist, or diabolical, or both. So far, he is speaking of the colleges. But in the University library itself Cox was "so zealous in purging this place of its rarities, especially such that had rubrics in them or any way savoured (as he thought) of superstition, that he left not one of those goodly manuscripts given by benefactors". One book only was restored by the time of an inquisition in Mary's reign. Some were burnt, others sold to booksellers or glovers, tailors or bookbinders; others kept by the reformers for themselves. The library room itself was put to infamous uses. Wood seems to go on no authority beyond the stories

handed down to him a century and a quarter after the supposed event. But he is followed, without question, by historians such as Gairdner and Dixon, who tell us that the Visitors
destroyed books and manuscripts with unexampled fury.
But is this altogether credible? Some purging of scholastic
theology is likely enough, if the earlier Visitors of 1535, who
had already filled the quadrangle of New College with leaves
of Duns Scotus, had left any. The burning of books with
which you did not agree was a favourite medieval method of
controversy, which survived long after multiplication by the
printing-press turned it into a gesture of protest rather than
an act of censorship. Oxford students of 1526 who had
copies of Tyndale's New Testament were made to go in
procession from St. Mary's to St. Frideswide's, and cast them
into a bonfire at Carfax by the way. Cuthbert Tunstall,
Bishop of London, even bought up copies of this book for the
express purpose of burning them, much to the "succour and
comfort" of Tyndale, who badly needed the money. Thomas
More had warned Tunstall that this would be so. As late as
1683 the political writings of Hobbes and Milton were
burnt by order of Convocation in the Schools quadrangle.
Wood's own *Athenæ* had a similar fate in 1693. If my memory
serves me, somebody thought it worth while to burn a copy
of *Robert Elsmere*.[1] What uncontrolled college hot-heads
may have done in 1550, one cannot say. But there was little
scholastic theology among Duke Humphrey's books. They
were primarily Latin classical manuscripts, to which Greek
ones had probably been added since Humphrey's time. It is
difficult to believe that they can have been deliberately
destroyed by the commissioners, whose statutes, printed by
Mr. Gibson, are sound enough on the educational side, and
lay especial stress on the teaching of Greek. Nor can literate
men, bishops and deans, really have been incapable in 1550
of distinguishing between one type of manuscript and
another. Wood's bit about red letters reads like an echo of the
scene in Shakespeare's *Henry VI*, where the Clerk of Chat-
ham is treated by Jack Cade as a conjuror, because he has a
book with red letters in his pocket. Certainly, however, Wood

[1] Or was it *Jude the Obscure*?

did not invent the tradition. Thomas Fuller twice refers to it before him. John Pitts may have known of it in 1619. And even in Bodley's time, Lady Dormer had been told that the books and shelves had been burnt, and Sir John Harington that Oxford had had a good library until a Cambridge man became Chancellor and cancelled our catalogue and scattered our books. He evidently meant Cox. On the other hand, a note by Archbishop Parker, to which I think Mr. Gibson first called attention, records a conversation of 1574 with Thomas Walley of Christ Church, who told him that, when he was Proctor in 1563, the library of the Divinity School was replenished—that is, in Elizabethan usage, filled rather than refilled—"with old Authors written, and with stalles and Deskes, on both sides Librarie wise, which weare taken awaie and solde to Christe Church theare". This is, of course, more like evidence than anything Wood gives us, and fits in with a University decree of 1566 for the sale of the benches, and with another note taken by Dr. Craster from a Selden manuscript of 1574 of some verses "found in an old book in the University library when it was transformed into the physics schools that now be". Here we have, perhaps, the "infamous uses" of which Wood speaks. The rather ambiguous record of a traveller from Basle in 1599 tells us that, after visiting the Bodleian, he saw the old library at New College. In any case the mystery of Humphrey's books remains unsolved, since no trace of them has been reported from Christ Church or New. Bodley, whose own memory would go back to 1563, speaks neither of a tragedy nor of a sale. He conceived that there was only a store of books without any allowance for increase or supply of those decayed, "whereby it came to pass, that when those that were in being were either wasted or embezzled, the whole foundation came to ruin".

Bodley's own ghost, the aspect of which would be familiar to us all from his portrait and bust, will follow Humphrey's. He, too, was an unsuccessful politician, tangled against his will in the intrigues of the Earl of Essex against the Cecils, who chose the better part of service in his elder years to the Oxford of his youth. I do not know whether I shall see William Shakespeare. We cannot believe him to have been a university man, although in so saying I run counter to the arguments of the ingenious writer who contributed an article on "Shakespeare at Corpus" to an early number of the *Pelican Record*. But a more imaginative biographer would point out to you that Lord Hunsdon, who was one of the first benefactors enlisted by Bodley, was the Lord Chamberlain under whom Shakespeare's company served, and that the poet would certainly have wished to pay respect to his patron by visiting the library; and further, that he had every opportunity for doing so, when he stayed with John Davenant and Mrs. Davenant at the house with the painted chamber in the Cornmarket, on his journeys between London and Stratford.

An early ghost for whom I shall certainly look out will be that of Sir Richard Lee, who gave the Bodleian some Russian manuscripts, and later bequeathed to it the famous Muscovy gown, supposed to be made of the skins of the vegetable lamb of Tartary, which may have been a tree-fern and may have been the cotton-plant, and shown to strangers in later days, when its origin was forgotten, as Joseph's coat of many colours. Sir Richard was an illegitimate brother of Sir Henry Lee of Ditchley, Queen Elizabeth's champion at the tilt. He made his fortune, sixteenth-century wise, partly by marrying widows richly left, and partly as a trader in the Muscovy Company. In 1600 he was sent on an embassy to Boris Godunof, Emperor of Muscovy, and to this belongs an episode, very characteristic of Elizabeth, which has not yet, I think, got into the history-books. The ostensible purpose of the mission was to secure commercial privileges for English subjects, which enabled an economical queen to charge its very considerable cost to the Company. But Elizabeth had been alarmed by a rumour that the Emperor's daughter was likely to marry an Austrian archduke, and Lee had secret instructions to propose as a counterbalance a match between the Emperor's son and a daughter of Ferdinando, late Earl of Derby. Godunof readily accepted the offer, but by the time of Lee's return next year either the royal purpose had veered, or, which is more likely, the lady's relatives had proved recalcitrant. A very similar thing had already happened in the days of Ivan the Terrible. A letter of apology was drafted, surely by Elizabeth's own hand. To her great grief, she would have the Emperor know, she had found that the boy and girl would be misgraffed in respect of years. He was only thirteen and she was eighteen. And so:

We have thought it our part by this letter to let you know how the case standeth, and to assure you that if we had any one of our blood (nay of our own body) answerable to your expectation, we would think ourself both honoured and strengthened by such a match. But as it hath pleased Almighty God so to dispose our mind, as it could never give way to those affections which might have been the means to raise an issue of our own person—a matter whereof we have no cause for our own mind to be sorry, but only because we perceive how infinitely our people would have been comforted, to be assured to have been left to no other's rule than such as should be derived from ourselves—we think it our part no longer to hold you in expectation.

And now the merchants took alarm. Such a rebuff would be the end to English trade in Muscovy. Probably the draft was modified. At any rate a letter of the following year announces that a suitable bride, unfortunately not named, had been found, and that an embassy would follow. But when the time came for the embassy, the affections of her subjects were no longer at Elizabeth's disposal. It was as well. Boris Godunof himself died a year or two later, the intended bridegroom was murdered, and the crown of Muscovy returned to the house of Ivan the Terrible.

Sir Richard Lee's Muscovy gown was a gift from the Emperor. On his return he concealed it from the Queen, who took his other curiosities without giving him a recompense, and kept it for the Bodleian. He came to the Encaenia of 1602, at which the formal opening of the library was originally to have taken place. But it was put off to 8th November, the day on which we still annually approach the familiar staircase, only to find it closed for the visitation of the Curators. And the Encaenia was notable only, says a contemporary letter-writer, for a great confluence of cutpurses, whereby Sir Thomas Bodley lost his cloak, and Sir Richard Lee two jewels of 200 marks, which he and Sir Henry meant to have bestowed on the bride, Mr. Tanfield's daughter. The offspring of this Oxford marriage was the famous Viscount Falkland of the Civil Wars.

James the First visited the Bodleian in 1605, but he is the least attractive of all our sovereigns, and I do not want to hear him repeating his plagiarized epigram that, if he had not been King of England, he would have wished to have been an Oxford student, or the other pedantic remarks which so annoyed Bodley that he dedicated the first edition of the catalogue to Prince Henry, instead of to his father. I would rather see Charles I, engaged with Falkland over the famous *Sortes Virgilianae*—if indeed that really took place in the Bodleian, which seems doubtful—wherein each saw his authentic fate foretold; or General Thomas Fairfax, whose first deed, when the City surrendered, was to set a guard upon the library, to save it from embezzling and cutting the chains of books, such as it had suffered from the cavaliers. But I shall not go into Selden End, to see it turned into a banqueting room for Fairfax and Cromwell, or for James II, who sat there alone before one hundred and eleven dishes of meat, sweetmeats, and fruit, while a crowd of hungry courtiers and academics waited until his rising gave the signal for a scramble, in which the wet sweetmeats were flung on the ladies' linen and petticoats and spoiled them. Anthony Wood might well have spoken of "infamous uses" here.

Attractive ghosts from the seventeenth century will be Casaubon, who read greedily for six hours a day in 1613, Andrew Marvell, a Cambridge man, whose name is in the registers of admission for 1665, and Anthony Wood himself, who notes the precise date of his coming to the library "which he took to be the happiness of his life, and into which he never entered without great veneration". "What with music, and rare books that he found in the library", he says elsewhere, "his life, at this time and after, was a perfect Elysium". After him will come Thomas Hearne, a mean little ink-stained figure, but an industrious worker, who, for all his Jacobite vapourings and his constant denigration of his contemporaries, did much to keep historical studies alive in evil times. The Bodleian, indeed, was not at its best during the earlier part of the eighteenth century, and I am afraid that there will be a bevy of ghosts, denied for ever the right of free access, and left moaning in a limbo at the top of the stairs, with Hearne, restored to the post of janitor, from which he was expelled in 1716, to keep guard over them. Here will be the idle and greedy librarians described by Von Uffenbach, one of whom is alleged to have thrown volumes bearing Milton's autograph inscriptions on a pile of duplicates for sale. Here, too, will be the unforeseeing librarian of a former day, who sold the First Folio of Shakespeare when the Third appeared, and cost earlier Friends of the Bodleian all that pain to redeem it for £3,000. Here, too, the pilferers and mutilators of books, and Constantine Simonides, that sly Greek, who tried to outwit Henry Octavius Coxe, and the forgers of Shakespearean documents, although from these the Bodleian has been comparatively free, unless indeed Dr. Tannenbaum is right in supposing that the descriptions of performances in 1611, ostensibly by the astrologer Simon Forman, are really the work of John Payne Collier. But that I do not believe.

Samuel Johnson returned to Oxford in 1754, a quarter of a century after he had been what he chose, for some reason, to call a "singing bird" at Pembroke. It was the first of several visits. He meant to work on his *Dictionary*, but did not do so, which was a pity, since we have learnt in our own day what excellent work can be done on a dictionary in the Bodleian. It was in the Trinity Library that he was sitting when he answered a critic of its narrowness—"Sir, if a man had a mind to *prance* he must study at All Souls and Christ Church". But for the Bodleian, too, that remark may have its wisdom. To the Bodleian he presented one of his books. It was *An Account of an Attempt to ascertain the longitude at Sea, by an exact variation of the Magnetic Needle*. It is not perhaps very much read now, except of course by Dr. Chapman and Mr. Powell. But Johnson was proud of it, and insisted on entering its title with his own hand in the Catalogue. It is difficult to imagine Johnson as a ghost, but I should certainly like to see for myself that ungainly figure in a brown tradesman's wig, and to hear for myself one of those annihilating half-truths.

The sentimental attitude to the Bodleian, already noticeable in Anthony Wood, made a natural appeal to the writers of the romantic revival. Oxford became almost a place of pilgrimage. Coleridge was there in 1794, on the fatal visit to Southey, which took him to Bristol and the fount and origin, as he afterwards thought, of all his woes. But he did not like the place. "Verily, Southey," he wrote, "thou art a nightingale among owls." He does not mention the Bodleian, but it would be odd if such a *helluo librorum* did not see it. The request, now so prominent at the entrance of Duke Humphrey's, to talk little, would not, I fear, have appealed to him. Wordsworth came, with his sister, in 1798, and saw the University, but seems to have been more impressed with the presence-chamber at Blenheim; and when Wordsworth was again at Oxford in 1839 to take an honorary degree, his letters describe nothing but the warmth of his own reception in the Sheldonian. Perhaps these ghosts will not be there. But I shall certainly see Charles Lamb, who came in 1800, and again with Hazlitt in 1810. Lamb was in his element. "He and the old colleges were hail-fellow well met; and in the quadrangles, he walked gowned." So Hazlitt tells us, and we may learn as much from Lamb's own Essay on " Oxford in the Vacation", although there the reminiscences are curiously mingled with others which belong to Cambridge.

What a place to be in is an old library! It seems as though all the souls of all the writers, that have bequeathed their labours to these Bodleians, were reposing here, as in some dormitory, or middle state. I do not want to handle, to profane the leaves, their winding sheets. I could as soon dislodge a shade. I seem to inhale learning, walking amid their foliage; and the odour of their old moth-scented coverings is fragrant as the first bloom of those sciential apples which grew amid the happy orchard.

But now a doubt assails me. How, beneath the phantasmal gown, will Charles Lamb be dressed? "I go in black" he says, and one would indeed expect some such accustomed livery of the India House. But hear Hazlitt again.

A little hunchbacked tailor was ordered to make a pair of brown or snuff-coloured breeches for my friend C— L—, instead of which the pragmatical old gentleman (having an opinion of his own) brought him home a pair of "lively lincoln-green", in which I remember he rode in Johnny Tremaine's cross-country caravan through Newbury and entered Oxford, "fearing no colors", the abstract idea of the jest of the thing prevailing in his mind (as it always does) over the sense of personal dignity.

There was plenty of motley in Lamb's brain, but to see motley on his legs in the Bodleian would be strange. With Lamb, of course, came Hazlitt himself. He, too, claims to have been "at home in the Bodleian". But I am not altogether sure that I want to encounter Hazlitt's scowl.

A singular link between the eighteenth and the nineteenth century was Routh, the President of Magdalen, again familiar to us all from his frail portrait upstairs. He must have known the Bodleian during most of his hundred years, and his famous advice to Dean Burgon, who had asked him for a maxim of life—"Sir, you will find it a very good practice always to verify your references, Sir"—ought surely to be framed in Duke Humphrey's opposite the request for silence. It was Routh who remembered Johnson's tradesman's wig, and he lived on into the days of Coxe, the good librarian, who never entered the room without looking at Bodley's portrait and resolving to do nothing that day which Sir Thomas would have disliked. And Coxe was a contemporary of our fathers. He was a friend of my own father, and I may have seen him myself, for my first visit to Oxford was about 1878, two or three years before Coxe's death. And since then the library has been the spiritual home of a long succession of scholars, passing on from hand to hand, like the runners of Marathon, the torch of learning, surely not to be quenched in the sea of modernity. Some there are among them whom we cannot yet think of as ghosts, when we are caught by the surprise of their empty chairs.

1935.

OXFORD REVISITED

For why should ghosts feel angered?
Let all their interference
Be faint march-music in the air.

UNDERGRADUATES are not generally philosophers; they are too much absorbed in the study of
Greats. None the less, it might be so that, in the long process
of time, one here and there should be afflicted with that
particular form of the scholar's melancholy, which is speculation. Surely it would be worth the while of such an one,
withdrawing himself from the strenuous life of the river and
the schools, to stand beneath the medieval city wall, and
contemplate *sub specie aeternitatis* the factors of his own
environment. But for the ordinary man the sweet influences
of Oxford only suffer analysis when they cease to be vital.
Absence quickly lends the perspective which philosophic
abstraction failed to attain. The characteristic notes of the
University, the wealth of historic tradition there, the old-
world setting of rare material beauty, discover themselves
most readily to the elect sojourner, not to the resident. And
let the visit be in vacation, in one of those protracted periods
of repose, when the insistent life of full term time is lulled,
and the colleges stand empty, monumental of the forces
which reared them. Elia, sympathetic soul, found Oxford
most kindly in vacation, and I avow myself of his thinking.

Alas! I am no longer an undergraduate: yet, only the
other day, a whimsical combination of circumstances led
me to return, under new conditions, to the precincts wherein
I had spent so many pleasant and perchance profitable years.
It was August, and the streets were filled with the fluttering
muslins and ardent faces of Extension Students. On them,
too, something of the indwelling spirit had alighted. I
paused for a moment at the door of the Bodleian, central
symbol of the city, and then sought its greener places. Here,
in the kingdom of the past, it seemed not inappropriate that

the pomps of Midsummer should be already giving way to the rich pageantries of autumn. Half-deserted gardens, a little overgrown, slept at the feet of darkening elms. Hollyhocks, of divers hues, blazed in the shadow of grey stonework; and on the northern border of the Parks stood a long company of mulleins, great flowering spikes, visible as a line of primrose far across the cricket ground. I traced again the windings of the twin streams. The broad shields of water-lilies, with here and there a white or golden blossom, lay on the clear pools of the Cherwell. Bronze dragon-flies darted from bank to bank, busy and irresponsible. A flood of emerald light poured through the leaves of overhanging willows, and a belated scent of hay came from the water-meadows, where they were still cutting the aftermath. Leaving the river-walks, I entered the vacant quadrangle of my old college. I trod familiar halls, which were no longer my home. In the rush of quite unacademic interests, I strove to recover the faded emotions of a not distant past. I remembered hours spent in converse with dear friends, in the rifling of countless books. Now the place seemed given over to the dead, and I was tingling with life. I felt myself a stranger here, another personality from the boy that was then. A few months before I had crept away from Oxford, a weary scholar, chagrined by defeat: now I came back renewed, strong in young hopes, refilled with the lust of living. But the first fine careless rapture of boyhood, does that ever return?

I stood in rooms that I had once inhabited; they had passed to some one else, of different tastes and habits from mine; but the sight of the chairs and tables awoke a curious sense of kinship, and beneath the windows the little college garden lay placidly as ever, with its hot smell of stocks and roses. Then I became aware that the rooms were full of ghosts. From the folds of the curtains, from empty bookcases and smoky ceiling they gathered to greet me. Some of them I knew well; I had often beheld them in the silences of the night. There are always spiritual presences in these old dusty college rooms: they look at you with friendly eyes, but you do not know their names. I could wish that some record were kept on each staircase of the successive generations of its occupants: it were a legitimate pride for reverent youth to boast of predecessors who achieved greatness, and a pleasure to shape the romance of those forgotten. But there were others in this shadowy company that seemed but alien phantoms among the rest: they were mine own. Ghosts of buried ideals and old ambitions, aspirations that I never realized and shall never want to realize, here where they were born and died, they stared at me reproachfully, relentlessly. Reminiscent of what was, they mocked the future with fear of change. Yet they were impotent. Truly it is not well to rake the ashes of the past; let the dead selves lie among their faded rose-leaves; yonder are the heights, this is the path; why linger to pluck cypress-boughs from the grave-yards in the valley?

Gladly I left them there, shut the oak upon them, and escaped into the sunshine.

1893.